THE

CHALLENGE

OF

INTERIOR

DESIGN

Professional Values and Opportunities

MARY V. KNACKSTEDT

11   10   09   08   07   5   4   3   2   1

Published by Allworth Press
An imprint of Allworth Communications, Inc.
10 East 23rd Street, New York, NY 10010

Cover design by Derek Bacchus
Interior design by Mary Belibasakis
Page composition/typography by Integra Software Services, Pvt., Ltd., Puducherry, India

Library of Congress Cataloging-in-Publication Data

Knackstedt, Mary V.
  The challenge of interior design: professional values and opportunities / Mary V. Knackstedt.
       p. cm.
Includes bibliographical references and index.
  ISBN-13: 978-1-58115-506-8 (pbk.)
  ISBN-10: 1-58115-506-9
1. Interior decoration—Practice.   2. Interior decoration—Marketing.
3. Vocational guidance.   I. Title.

  NK2110.K546 2008
  729.068—dc22

                                                      2007042384

Printed in the United States of America

CONTENTS

TODAY'S CLIENTS 56

Demographics • Marketing to Generations X and Y • Changed Incomes • The Way We Live • What Do Clients Want? • Forging the Link • User-Friendly Design Studios • Areas of Influence

DESIGN FIRMS 71

Patterns of Success • The Information Gap • The Way We Work • Style of Our Firms • Mystique Versus Value • Interior Design is an Art and a Science • Finance

A MISSION FOR THE INTERIOR DESIGN FIELD 87

Innovation • Taking Responsibility for Healthy Environments • Design Affects Behavior • Responsibility to Keep Learning • Designers as Agents of Change • Mission Statements

SYSTEM OF THINKING 107

Change • Redesign from the Roots Up • Values • Ethics • Responsibility • Judgment • Vision and Purpose • Power • Image • It's Hard to Change Your System of Thinking

LEARNING PROGRAMS 137

Keep On Learning • Redesigning Design Education

COMMUNICATE 152

Persuasive Power of Design • Problem-Solving • The Designer-Client Relationship • Speaking • Industry-Wide Communications Efforts • Listening • Communication Tools

THE DESIGN TEAM 166

Defining the Team • Leadership • Consultants on Call • What Makes a Good Team Member? • Handling Organizational Conflicts

INTRODUCTION

Interior design is an important profession and one to which its practitioners are seriously dedicated. We know that interior design can do a great deal to change the world, whether in people's homes or in public spaces. However, designers work independently so often that we don't always have the opportunity to share in what other designers are doing.

Fortunately, through the many practices represented in our Designers' Business Forum, a program I developed to help designers, architects, and other creative professionals take advantage of today's business environment, I have had the opportunity to go "inside" other design firms throughout the country. I realize the value of what designers do. We have incredible power and opportunity. We have a chance to make the world a better place and we're doing it one room at a time. You're part of this change, and, as such, are very important to the future of society.

Our field has undergone a lot of changes. We don't understand all of them and we wonder where we belong. We realize we can't do business exactly the way we have been doing it. We've also seen some of our major sources leave the field, and we've had to adjust accordingly. Adjusting isn't easy. We often question change; and yet, as designers, we are creators of change.

Interior design affects everyone. It has the power to direct movement and interaction, enhance vision and hearing, and inspire emotion. It is taken for granted even by the people who practice it. Interior design has been and always will be practiced in partnership with other disciplines, but through their work, interior designers orchestrate what these related disciplines do.

With the right environment, interior design can make it possible for people to do better at whatever they attempt. Great things can happen as a result of good design. Bad design, or lack of design, can contribute to serious problems, even social unrest. Good design makes people's movements more effective and their lives more comfortable and pleasurable. Social scientists have documented many things we interior designers instinctively know about the way people respond to their environments, whether it's a baby in a nursery or adults in a crowded auditorium.

Most interior designers regard this power, and the responsibility that comes with it, too casually. I am not sure the term "interior design" is strong enough to convey the responsibility of our profession.

It's time to acknowledge that interior design has evolved and can affect the way we live like no other profession. We have the training to accept this responsibility. Our work has the potential to change the way people live for generations. We can create living spaces that are healthier, support a range of human activities better, and inspire behavior that is more socially acceptable. What a challenge, and what an exciting profession we work in!

I speak from experience. I was born into this industry and have spent more than thirty years working in the design field, both as a designer and as a business consultant to other designers. This broad exposure to the effects of design work has taught me to respect the potential of the field.

I am also an optimist and an instigator. Seeing the potential of interior design, I want us all to benefit from it. Interior design today is a whole new game, and it's thrilling.

MARY V. KNACKSTEDT

CHAPTER 1

TODAY'S DESIGN WORLD IS DIFFERENT

Reasonable men adapt themselves to their environment; unreasonable men try to adapt their environment to themselves. Thus all progress is the result of the efforts of the unreasonable man.

—GEORGE BERNARD SHAW

The interior design field has seen many changes in the past fifteen or twenty years. The 1990s created a completely different set of opportunities, removing some and bringing others to fruition. Now that we've moved into a new century, we see even more opportunities and some really beautiful and exciting things happening. It's not just merchandise being made all over the world; it's also our ability to communicate with and work with talented individuals around the globe. A single item of furniture might incorporate several different components and the work of many different international craftspeople. We're able to produce products we never even thought of in the past and to bring many new opportunities to domestic as well as foreign markets. This is really a dramatic change.

Fortunately, as designers, we love creating new things, and we enjoy and need change. Many of the changes that have been forced upon us have actually proven to be of great benefit. We have seen a transformation. I'm sure we'll see even more. But the

1

wonderful thing that has come out of these changes is that design-ers have had the opportunity to really show and use their talents. We've discovered new ways of working and new systems we never thought possible. As a result of these changes, we're able to bring a much better end product to our clients.

CHANGING BUSINESS MODELS, EXPANDING PURPOSE AND MEANING

Our industry is not the only one in transition. Theories on business management pop up faster than you can say "total quality management," "reengineering the corporation," or "rethinking the corporation." Thank goodness these theories have taken the place of other strategies for success, which include intimidation and manipulation. In the recent past, so many businesses focused on the next quarter's profits; now they are beginning to pay attention to the reason they're in business in the first place.

Winston Churchill said, "We make a living by what we get. We make a life by what we give." We'll be looking more at what we give in this next decade—what we give to our clients, our colleagues and collaborators, our community, and to the world.

This will remind us of the reasons we are in this industry. We have worked hard to be efficient and profitable. Some of the sys-tems used by businesses have sapped our dedication to our work, and we have lost something vital in our struggle to survive.

Now we have an opportunity to find purpose and meaning in our work. For our profession to be as rewarding as it ought to be, our value system must be the basis for setting priorities. We have to combine an accurate picture of the current realities with our vision for our profession and the world.

There are trends our industry can't ignore, both nationwide and global. Downsizing and technology have cut the workforce and changed the way people work. There is a new decentraliza-tion of power and an increase in cooperative efforts. An estimat-ed twenty-four million Americans now work at home.

Consumer awareness and concern for energy-efficient pro-ducts, protecting the environment, and indoor air quality have pushed manufacturers in a new direction. The issue of sustainabil-ity is strong. Even more than that, we're into zero-energy-based building. The ADA, Americans with Disabilities Act, is everywhere. We can't think of designing any space or product without considering it.

Every part of our life is affected by technology. All of our communication systems permit us to work in a very global fashion. This was never possible before. Services such as international telephones and all forms of computers have changed everything, including our government, banking, engineering, and drafting systems. Now a designer can work from Japan in collaboration with someone in the United States, so we are working at all times of day and night in order to communicate one-on-one.

Shopping online has made 800 numbers a thing of the past; the Internet is one of the fastest-growing businesses in our industry. We thought it was only the 800 numbers that were our competition, but now the visual presentation of items online is even more enticing. I was amazed to hear that a person in our neighborhood who did not sleep well, would log on to eBay and purchase as much as $25,000 worth of products in a single night. This is probably just the beginning of what we can expect in the years to come.

Douglas MacArthur said, "There is no security on this earth. There is only opportunity." We have an opportunity to change our field, to put the heart and soul and passion back into it, to fulfill our desire to make people's lives better through design. It takes a great deal of dedication, a strong core belief, and a willingness to play the game and to take on the responsibility.

Large companies usually have a definite structure based on production and appropriate financial return. Often, this structure is not complementary to the creative spirit of designers. The litigious world we live in has forced architects and designers to do repetitive work, rather than exert their creative effort as much as they'd like. They're afraid of legal suits that may result if they try something new. Both the financial requirements of corporations and our litigious world often take the creativity out of our work.

Rereading *Reengineering the Corporation*,[1] I thought about how it applied to our field. Interior design is both an art and a science: it has developed into something far more complex than choosing fabric and colors. We need to recognize that design encompasses a broad range of activities and a great many responsibilities.

Reengineering the Corporation emphasizes that businesses should examine current conditions and the needs of current clients. So many of the traditions of our field, the way we always practiced, are just not suitable to today's circumstances. Technology has remarkably changed our work. Technology has also permitted us to bring specialists in from other parts of the world to work with us. This would never have been possible before. We are often asked to provide expertise in areas that were not typically part of the interior design field in the past. Like other companies that follow the reengineering principles, interior designers need to review client interaction, staffing sources, and everything else that affects business today. We have already reengineered our field in many different ways—and we will have to make even more changes in the future.

I have worked in this field a long time. I'm not going to throw away everything I've learned since design school. I'm going to keep redesigning my business so that the process is even more productive and enjoyable. I'm constantly asking questions and looking at new directions. I know I don't have all the answers, but I hope this book will encourage interior designers to see opportunities and the power we have. We are agents for change in the world.

THE FUTURE IS THE PAST

Many observers have attributed the change in business ethics to spiritual awakening of the baby boomers. It seems to me that the bright promise of the future is really a return to the good old standards of the past. The values that existed before all the manipulative formulas for success came into fashion will be reasserted, and teamwork along with a sense of responsibility will be the model. No matter what you call it, there is a new and stronger emphasis today on relationships and responsibility.

This emphasis permits us to deal with real values. As Americans grow more and more sensitive to the environment and what our mistreatment of it costs us, we will act as stewards rather than consumers. Long-term efficiency will be valued over short-term profit, both in business and in our personal lives. In other words, we should examine our actions in terms of what will be healthful and helpful to people who work with us, our clients, and the world. We'll be looking to nature as a partner. We won't have to fight the sun and moisture levels, because our designs will work with them.

New patterns of business affect the way we work today. In the past, many designers worked in large groups for one corporation. Now, many of us are employed independently in one city, or we team up with other designers in a very distant city. The whole structure of the design field, like that of many other fields, is different. This permits designers to be more independent. Designers who are night people can work at night. If they have children, they can arrange their schedules around family. They can incorporate other parts of their lives into their daily schedules in a more harmonious fashion. On the other hand, independent designers are also forced to take on more responsibilities. When designers worked for others, they had a superior who oversaw their work and corrected mistakes. Today, we are much more responsible for what we do.

The scale of business has returned to a more human dimension. In order to produce high-quality work and have better control, firms are using fewer resources and often smaller staffs. Staff members are changing many of their procedures in order to keep up with the market. Technology gives us the opportunity to bring in high-level staff people from almost anywhere in the world. They are not on our weekly payrolls, yet they are still a part of our company. Even global firms look different. Often global corporations are made up of many small firms. Each division performs independently but is linked, as states are to the federal government.

Accounting systems are changing. It's not simply a matter of cash assets, return on investment, or short-term profits. To meet the challenges of our changing industry, we need knowledge and people with ability.

The wealth of a company is not necessarily limited to the building it owns or its physical assets. Rather, "wealth" incorporates social accounting—the way people get along, not only with contacts in their Rolodexes but also with their work teams. These teams might be made up of professionals from many different areas. It isn't just dollars and cents, but people. When staff are ready, available, and used to working together, a business can move forward on a project effectively. It's really social accounting and social skills that are so valuable today.

PEOPLE POWER

Today, a company must be more than its capital assets and equipment. It is intellectual capital that counts. Workers are a prime asset; having a well-qualified team of in-house staff, consultants, and resources is essential. Equipment becomes obsolete, sometimes within months or days or hours. People are the power that grows the firm. It's people who are resourceful and creative. Their talent is directed into earnings, whereas an obsolete piece of equipment is just so much junk you have to pay someone to haul away.

People want to work in a world where they see value. Making money is less important than being part of the creation of something with real value. Interior designers want to create environments that not only meet needs, but are exciting and something to be proud of.

Time is a key factor. We want to invest our time in something we see as worthwhile.

Futurists tell us that business will emerge as a leader of society responsible for the whole world. In the past, other social institutions were responsible. Today, businesses—especially small businesses—and business organizations stand the greatest chance of being able to make changes.

We used to think it would be wonderful to own a car or a house. But maybe too much ownership takes away some of our freedom, flexibility, and opportunity to do other things. Perhaps having seven cars and six houses may require more management than it's worth.

Ownership is an obligation, and in the future we will need to be more cautious about how we dedicate our obligations. Do we dedicate ourselves to a possession or to an opportunity? Do we want to spend our lives owning things or enjoying great adventures?

We should address not only what we want, but what our clients want. To take it a step further, we should look at not just what we think clients want, but what they need. Change is one thing that will be constant. With the benefit of technology and a flexible structure of professional firms around the world, we can manage these changes easily and meet the needs of clients more efficiently.

The terms that keep popping up again and again in discussion of this topic are "relationships," "specialization," "focus," and "self-motivation." Many of the old terms that were part of our practice will be replaced by these and other new terms.

A company is not strictly an interior design firm. In most instances it has a specialty or two complementary specialties. Very few firms consider themselves "generalists" today. When you think of what we actually do, whether it's turnkey operations or creating a branding image, we produce specific projects that serve particular needs. We don't just make everything neat and pretty.

The greatest privilege anyone can give us is the opportunity to do challenging work, to create within our discipline, and to use our enthusiasm and the skills of our profession. Considering the expanding opportunities, what a challenge!

Notes

1. Michael Hammer and James Champy. *Reengineering the Corporation: A Manifesto for Business Revolution.* New York: Harper Business, 1993.

CHAPTER 2

A PASSION FOR DESIGN

I don't know a real designer who works only for a paycheck. Every one of us wants to be doing something we believe in. There is the excitement that comes from being a part of a special project. There is the visible result. We're happy to be going to work every morning. It's not a case of getting up and thinking, "I've got to be there by 8:30." We all eagerly anticipate going to work because once we get there we are working on something worthwhile. Each project can be worthy of our talent and effort.

Not everyone is totally self-motivated, but if they are part of an exciting project, they become motivated. They get caught up in the excitement of it. Most designers like to talk about their work. They are excited to tell you what they're doing. They are passionate. They're enthusiastic. They're committed to what they do. Interior design is definitely more than a job—it's really a mission, an excitement, a religion. There is no greater natural high.

THE DESIGN SPIRIT

It's time to recognize the value of interior design. Interior designers know what design can do. We're excited by it. We are willing to exert every effort required to give our clients the special environments that will permit them to perform with greater ease and enjoyment. This is the core, the soul, the mission of interior design. It is the understanding of and belief in that mission that gives design new spirit.

I see this spirit, this energy, in chapter after chapter of design organizations, from design center to design center, throughout this country. I have now conducted workshops in all but four states and have seen many different styles of

8

practicing interior design. Although the process and style of work often differ due to client, climate, or geography, this spirit, attitude, and excitement form a common denominator. Interior designers share the belief that the world is going to be a better place because they have been here. You see this spirit in successful design centers and design firms. When the spirit is gone, the firm seems dead.

The role designers play often varies depending on the personal styles and wishes of different clients and the type of project we're working on. Some clients want you to create a space that gives them a different experience, a space that stimulates them to do different things and live in different ways. In many cases, clients will simply state their objectives, and it's the responsibility of the designer to make them happen. Often these clients know the designer's work, and they have great confidence in what the designer is doing. They want that designer to be totally responsible for the design, and to do it according to the very highest standards. In such instances, design is totally under the control of the designer. This obviously isn't true in every situation. Some clients like to participate.

DESIGNER AS COACH/TRAINER

Today almost everyone believes he or she is an interior designer, just as there are people who believe they know how to exercise and people who exercise with personal trainers. Professional trainers help people spend exercise time wisely, resulting in well-shaped bodies. In the same way, interior designers can be coaches, helping clients meet their design needs.

These clients want control over their own lives and environments. In these cases, interior design is performed in partnership with the client—a partnership similar to that between a coach or personal trainer and an athlete or client. A design trainer assists individuals, companies, and associations by expanding their opportunities and exposing them to experiences, materials, and techniques they may have never seen. This improves the quality of the project.

Design can profoundly affect many aspects of a client's environment. It can improve health and comfort with furnishings that support physical needs. Design techniques can create specific psychological effects. Your work as a designer/trainer may include giving clients the opportunity to express their heritage, business motto, or social attitude.

Both the design client and the interior design professional must accept the responsibility of their positions and play their roles accordingly. Design is a refined discipline, not a helter-skelter process. It is too easy to be led down a blind alley. Good communication between designer and client enhances the project. Focusing on the project and sharing information to achieve the common goal of a good design can be a spiritual experience; it can result in projects that symbolize the best of the art and science of interior design.

As designers we have the opportunity and skills to create spaces that interact with their inhabitants. So much in life is beyond our control. With interior design, we can create controlled environments. We need to take this responsibility seriously and to create spaces for our clients that complement their personalities and enhance the activities they will perform in these spaces.

THE CHALLENGE

Fortunately, many businesses operate more efficiently in a time of change than other social institutions because they're focused and productive. A business can adapt to change faster and more easily than many academic or government institutions, for example. Many nonbusiness institutions have a structure of status issues and entitlement. There are always exceptions, but generally businesses are more effective at change.

One of the areas in which we must bring all of these qualities into play is in our treatment of the people we hire and the people with whom we work. We can no longer afford to look at people as if they were easily replaceable and in need of constant supervision. We have to look at people in terms of potential, as team players who may become masters, designers, and leaders of teams. We must develop our team players into master performers.

Ownership alone is unfulfilling. Today many well-educated and brilliant people, people who are apparently successful, are looking for meaning in their lives. Joy in working is a major component of life. It's what made us designers. If we no longer enjoy designing, we have lost a great deal of our excitement in life.

We have to look at the true meaning of our profession. We have the ability to improve the lifestyles of our clients and others we come into contact with. In the past, many firms became so focused on high volume and production that the pressure made design no longer fun.

When your main purpose of being in business is to make money, you can't attain the performance levels possible when you're in business because you love it. In the past few decades we have been consumed with economic production and acquisition. Most businesses have been guided by what affects their corporations in the next quarter.

There are many ways of producing interiors projects; some of those have become routine. There are companies that have standardized products for open-office plans that are all the same, composed completely of elements that have been seen before. There are catalogs featuring many types of residential furnishings from which you can buy an entire room. In some cases, the furnishings have been mass-produced inexpensively, while in other cases, they are high-priced. Whatever the situation, decorating through catalogs has become routine. This is not what our clients are looking for. They don't want repetitious or ordinary things—they want the unusual.

WHAT ABOUT THE CASH?

There is a book entitled *Do What You Love, The Money Will Follow.*[1]

The truth is that enthusiasm and good feelings are attractive and contagious. If you love your work and show it, people are drawn to you and your business.

Recently I went into a restaurant on a Saturday night, a popular night for eating out in my town. The place was almost empty. Another restaurant was so busy no tables were available. What was the story? The food at the first restaurant is good; the service is good. The owner learned the restaurant business at the knee of his father, who has been very successful at every restaurant he ever ran.

His father had little formal education. The son went to college, and then decided to go into the restaurant business because he saw how successful his father had been. The son has an MBA from a noted university and figured he'd be a millionaire in no time. But the son has owned several restaurants, and not one of them has been a goldmine.

The explanation is that the father is in the business because he loves it. Two months ago, he bought a restaurant that wasn't doing well. It was producing $3,500 a week in gross sales. In less than a month, the father had the restaurant doing that amount of business in a day. The son and his father have totally different personalities. The son went into the business for the bottom line. His father is in it because he loves to serve great food and enjoys the social contact.

The point is that if you worry too much about the financial aspects of the work, it gets in the way. You cannot be worrying about the payroll on Thursday or Friday afternoon. You have to feel comfortable enough with finances to be able to concentrate on design and manage the rest of the business. When money becomes more important than anything else, it is a stressor. You can lose your creativity, your excitement, and your ability to produce.

In every course I've led and in my other books, I've tried to make managing a company comfortable to a designer. Even though I wrote a lot about money, the message was to be comfortable with it.

KEEP YOUR EYES ON REALITY

You cannot profit from the opportunities of a changing market unless you recognize current needs. These are thrown in front of us daily by newspapers, television, and the Internet. Although the situation seems overwhelming, great things are possible if you work on one small area at a time. Keep your eye on the reality of today as well as on the future. If you don't understand reality, you cannot make good, timely decisions. Here's an example. The nearly constant improvements in technology provide an opportunity for increased economy and efficiency. In some offices, we used to allow a certain amount of square footage for computers. That is no longer necessary.

Now we can allow for less space. A lot of paper storage needs have been reduced. Technology has changed the demands upon interiors. At one time everything had to be hard-wired and therefore within a certain distance of the main terminal. So much today is wireless. In medicine, the in patient versus out patient ratio has changed completely, thereby altering the requirements for hospital facilities. Security demands and almost every part of our lifestyles have also changed.

Look at what's real, what affects you, and the parameters of your decisions. Many designers apparently haven't really been dedicated to their work. We've been encouraged to look at what our work can do for us—to see how little time we can spend doing it and how little effort we can put into it. Unfortunately, we've been taking the easy way out, accepting cookie-cutter solutions rather than doing great design. The easy way is not exciting, fun, or innovative. We need to do better for our clients and for ourselves. It's not enough to have skills or talent; design demands dedication as well.

YOUR ENTHUSIASM INDEX

Remember how excited you were when you started out as a designer? The passion you had? Do you still have it?

It's a good idea to look at your career and review essential issues every six months:

- Are you passionate and excited about what you're doing? Do you get as much fun out of it as you used to? Does it still turn you on? Is this really what you want to be doing?
- Are you achieving your goals and objectives? Is this what you thought you wanted to do?
- If your objectives have changed, have they changed in the right direction?
- Is this a job for you, or is it a career? Does it meet your expectations?
- Are you really doing what you're good at, or are you spending too much time doing things you don't enjoy and aren't good at? If that time and energy had been spent on design, would it have enriched your design work and made you feel better about your career?

- What are the rewards? Do you have the satisfaction, excitement, joy, and rewards you want from this career?
- Is this where you want to be? Is this where you belong?
- Are you growing as a designer?

Remember that the smile in your voice and the bounce in your step are what clients find attractive.

Great designers are alight with creative energy. If you're not happy with what you are doing and the way it's going, do something about it. Stop—don't spend one more day agonizing. When you became a designer, you were dedicated and loved design. You still love design. There's something wrong with the *process* you are using to do your work. This can be corrected, and you can proceed to do even greater work and love it. There are so many examples of this among members of our Designers' Business Forum who found new life through new processes and the examples of others.

Attitude

In the book *The Difference Maker*,[2] John Maxwell points out that there's a great deal of difference between someone who has experience and someone with a good attitude. You can't make up for a lack of skill with a good attitude, and you can't make up for a bad attitude with skill and experience. We really need people with both.

Notes

1. Marsha Sinetar. *Do What You Love, The Money Will Follow: Discovering Your Right Livelihood.* New York: Paulist Press, 1986.
2. John C. Maxwell. *The Difference Maker: Making Your Attitude Your Greatest Asset.* Nashville: Nelson Business, 2006.

Chapter 3

BUSINESS THEORIES AND THEIR EFFECT ON THE WORKPLACE

*It is the nature of man as he grows older
to protest against change, particularly
change for the better.*

— John Steinbeck

In the introduction, we spoke about the changes in our industry. There were systems in place that we had been using for 200 years, but now we have replaced them with new ones. Some of the standards we thought were key are not at all appropriate to what we are doing today. We have a completely different division of labor. At one time, for example, computer-aided design work was done only by a technician; now there is a CAD system on everyone's desktop. We are communicating drawings and details through the Internet with precision that would never have been possible even a decade ago.

It is incredible to see just where we are, how it affects every decision we make, and our whole style of working. We really need to examine, on a regular basis, the processes required to complete an appropriate project. We need to examine the most efficient systems of today—not the ones of the past—that should be incorporated into that project.

TRADITIONAL SYSTEM

A strong system of control and accountability—the chain of command—was once part of the division of labor. The main advantage of this division of labor was that people could be trained quickly in one or two processes. Doing a single thing repetitively was supposed to make a person better and faster at the task. Everyone was accountable through a bureaucratic system.

The division of labor system has shaped the structure of management and performance in American businesses since 1776. A person could go to work for a company in his twenties and gradually be promoted to vice president with a corner office. This was the model for all business, whether it was factories, stores, utilities, or design firms. Division of labor reduced the cost of goods.

There were built-in disadvantages as well as advantages to this system. As instructions filtered down the chain of command, errors could occur at each level. Because no one saw the whole picture, and each area understood only its own function, the errors weren't recognized until the end. It would have been less expensive to fix them earlier in the process.

Over the years, production became systematized so one person could do many things; we didn't need as much management. Mergers and acquisitions—combining company structures—were other attempts to decrease administrative costs. The belief was that the processes learned in one field would apply to all, and that one executive could head several types of companies.

Mergers and acquisitions were tried in the home furnishings and design industry. However, in our field, merger mania, leveraged buy-outs, and conglomerates destroyed many companies. For example, Dolly Madison bought companies such as Dunbar. Dolly Madison knew the food business but not the furniture business. Many wonderful, small furniture companies have been bought by corporations from different industries who saw the purchases as good opportunities. These acquisitions turned out to be disasters due to the new owners' lack of understanding of the businesses they had bought.

There was a boom of independent businesses after World War II. Many of our soldiers brought back crafts they had seen in Europe and began opening factories here. This increased the volume of the design business tremendously. Soldiers also took advantage of the G.I. Bill, which allowed people to get an education and to improve their stations in life. A person could become an architect, whereas his or her father may have been a factory worker. This would have never been possible before. Better jobs, a booming economy, and lots of new young families led to an increased demand for furnishings and various products.

At this point, many of these people are older and would like to be out of the business. Many of them sold their businesses for good profits. Many of the buyers had a lot of money—far more money than the businesses had ever previously seen. Many of them were able to invest in and do great things with the businesses. However, others who didn't really understand the businesses they bought did disastrous things. They weren't the right people to run the businesses.

SEARCHING FOR AN ANSWER

Books on new theories of business management began to appear in the late 1980s: benchmarking, liberation management, I-Power, Total Quality Management, servant-leader, and reengineering. What they have in common is an emphasis on communication, respect, applied intelligence, and teamwork. They all eliminate layers of supervisors. But the biggest change is in the value system.

Reengineering the Corporation[1] tells us to ignore what is and concentrate on what could be. Reengineering, as authors Hammer and Champy describe it, is "the fundamental rethinking and radical redesign of the business process to achieve dramatic improvements in critical contemporary measures of performance, such as costs, quality, service, and speed."

Total Quality Management (TQM) is a popular management theory dedicated to improving the present process. Reengineering asks the question, is the present process worth saving? This is the question many corporations faced in the late 1980s. The result was downsizing and decentralization into smaller corporations and more independent entities.

Leadership consultant Joe Batten makes the point that TQM, as it is currently practiced, often is rigid and doesn't involve the entire organization.

Employee suggestion programs build a sense of community. I-Power, a program based on those suggestions, concentrates on small changes made by individuals. The office furniture firm of Haworth saved an estimated $8.2 million, based on 13,000 ideas from employees in 1993.[2]

Open-space meetings are a version of management by team.[3] Anyone with a passion about any company-related issue writes that issue at the top of a large piece of paper and tacks it to the bulletin board in the meeting space. Other employees then sign up for a discussion group about each issue. In each discussion group, the chairs are placed in a circle. A one-day session lays the groundwork for interdepartmental communication. A three-day meeting is needed when the company wants employees to form groups to carry out their ideas. This system of participatory management is still key in many firms.

VALUE OF PEOPLE

We mentioned this in chapter 1, but it deserves more examination here. Today the value of a company is the value of the people, not of the building or the price of the equipment. These people sell, they design, they manufacture, and they provide services. If a company is not doing as well as it could, it's probably because its people are not performing one of these functions as well as they could.

Businesses need to ask basic questions: What really works? What do clients want? How can we eliminate waste and work that doesn't add value?

Many traditional jobs have become simplified to the point that technology does most of the work faster and more accurately than people. The job of bookkeeper was once a very important position and generally took a full-time employee in even a small firm. That work is now done in a few hours and very often by those who are actually working on the project. Now we have more accountability for a lot less effort.

Today, task-oriented jobs are obsolete at many firms. For example, with the use of the right software program, bookkeeping can be done in almost any location in greater detail than an individual bookkeeper could ever do. CAD work is done and sent over the Internet. In the past, the same work would have required hand drafting and physically transporting large sets of prints. It's done so simply now. Specialists who did only CAD work usually find their jobs obsolete. They may have to become more like architects or designers—and take a second or third job in addition to CAD. CAD is often used by designers themselves, rather than by CAD specialists.

It's been amazing to see the number of high-quality furniture products in various markets that are American made. We thought the market was moving to other countries because of inexpensive labor. But we're finding that with technology, a lot of it is coming back to our own country—bringing many opportunities for designers working with manufacturers.

TODAY'S BUSINESS AND THE MARKET FOR INTERIOR DESIGN

Today's business is different. The prevailing mood of the 1990s was to make companies lean, responsive, competitive, efficient, and innovative. Just as design tasks have changed, so has the production process. For example, in the past, companies might have outsourced certain tasks, which they now find can be done more efficiently internally. Another change has been the downsizing of business. Small companies can move quickly. As a result, many companies have become smaller and more independent. Many people no longer work for a salary, but are consultants or part-time employees.

The market for office design, which made up a large percentage of our business in the past, shrank. This market no longer consists of multiple floors of desks, chairs, and landscape cubicles. The equipment of today takes up less room. Now the demands are different. There's a demand for expressive environments to produce desired communication.

New Work Styles

The new work styles affect all of us. Many companies allow employees to work at home two days a week and come to the office for only three. Other employees go to their formal offices only once a week or month to check in or have group conferences.

In addition, the changing demands in many fields have impacted interior design. Many medical institutions now encourage family members to stay with patients in the medical center, which requires these centers to be much more home-like in design. The minute we change any operation or design of any organization, it automatically means that the interior design requirements also change.

Allowing people to do their best work means designing workspaces that take advantage of natural human inclinations.

The office space of the future will be designed for flexibility, that is, for constantly changing groups of two or three, as the process demands. This is not a new concept; it has been around since the late 1960s.

With personal computers, modems, and faxes that fit in briefcases, people can work anywhere. Technophiles are calling this telecommuting the "virtual workplace," a take-off on virtual reality.

Jay Chiat, president of the four-hundred-person advertising agency Chiat/Day, compares traditional offices to kindergartens in which only two hours of work are done per day.[4] Chiat says he gives his staff the freedom to be more creative and more responsive to clients. Employees work out of their homes or in the offices of the clients. Chiat supplies employees with a personal computer, a dedicated telephone line, and some furniture. He believes this "virtual agency" will elevate the quality of work his firm produces.

In Manhattan, a 275-member accounting firm devoted one floor to the "officeless" office cubicles whose potential occupants must make a reservation to use the space.[5] A concierge keeps employee profiles with preferred office and floor locations. Within fifteen minutes of reserving a space, the employee's nameplate goes up outside the cubicle, his or her phone number and e-mail address are activated, and files are placed on the desk. The majority of the firm's consultants have traditional offices. This setup encourages people who should be doing most of their work on the road to get out on the road.

What is good for one isn't necessarily good for all. Some people become more autonomous and love working without being tied to an office. Others hate it and move to another structure.

A handful of companies hotel their office and cubicle spaces. Hoteling decreases real estate costs—sometimes by half—but critics say it merely underscores the impermanence of the employer/employee relationship. Charles O'Reilly, a professor at Stanford University's Graduate School of Business, says, "You're sending some very clear signals to people that they're simply an extension of some sort of machine."[6]

Magazines call people who carry their office in a briefcase "road warriors." Hotels cater to the business traveler. They now offer in-room Internet connection, enhanced lighting, fax machines, and office centers. Some hotels have a surcharge for this service, but in many cases it is included in your daily rate.

The rise in home-based businesses has created many opportunities for real estate developers. There are many combined residential and business spaces, allowing areas for work centers as well as shared conference rooms and other support business services. Zoning laws have changed in some locations to permit working and living in the same area; there was a time when zones restricted spaces to serve either residential or business purposes.

The downside to having the technical facilities to be able to work anytime and anyplace is that some people work fifty- to sixty-hour weeks. This may be because they have equipment with them and a free moment or they are simply unable to disengage from working—not because employers actually demand these hours.

In the 1970s, futurists told us that computers meant we would have paperless offices; we've learned this is not true—but technology has brought unexpected, radical changes to our workspaces. With today's technology, an office can be anywhere—in a park, on a boat, in our residence or in any part of the world. When we speak or interact with someone, we don't necessarily have any idea where they are. As a result, we all have options.

Companies have grown smaller, and many firms are realizing they need a strong team. Some groups come together as an official structured corporation, while others form a joint venture system. The idea of picking people up as needed doesn't always work because today's market forces us to work at an all-around high level of quality, efficiency, and speed. We really need to know whom we're working with and to be sure the team members are capable of carrying out the various responsibilities. We need high-level skills, flexibility, and speed.

Notes

1. Michael Hammer and James Champy, *Reengineering the Corporation: A Manifesto for Business Revolution.* New York: Harper Business, 1993, p. 32.
2. "Haworth Employees Save Company $," *The Monday Morning Quarterback,* June 26, 1994, p. 2.
3. Claudia H. Deutsch. "Round Table Meetings With No Agendas, No Tables," *New York Times,* June 5, 1994, p. 5.
4. *Monday Morning Quarterback,* July 1993, p. 2.
5. Phil Patton. "The Virtual Office Becomes Reality," *New York Times,* October 28, 1993, p. C1:5.
6. Mary Kane. "It's a Brave New Corporate Space," *Harrisburg Patriot,* June 13, 1994, p. B2.

Chapter 4

INDUSTRY

Once there was a "mystique" surrounding the home furnishing and design industry, and that was an asset. Clients had no idea where we got our items, which often were very hard to find. We would buy them from unusual sources in offbeat communities and bring them together, creating magic. Today, with the Internet and other systems of communication, clients know a lot more about where almost everything comes from. A lot of the mystique is gone.

At the same time, research indicates that consumers are confused by the massive amount of products available. They are overloaded with undifferentiated information.

With the items we once obtained for them being copied at much lower prices, consumers are questioning our integrity. They see us as elitists. This is really working against us. To maintain the respect of the public, we need to provide clear and specific information and make our field more user-friendly. Young people are attracted to transparency.

AN INDUSTRY IN CHAOS

I would estimate that in the 1990s, approximately 25 percent of all the furniture manufacturers and retailers in America felt the industry was in serious trouble. That is about twice the number who felt that way in the 1980s. Today, industry pessimists outnumber optimists, because they're still trying to do business as they did many years ago. They're not willing to change.

That we are in trouble may be the only thing the industry agrees on. The home furnishings and design industry is made up of literally hundreds of crafts, each with its own language and standards. As one industry observer commented, it's the only industry in which the branches don't share information. In general, our industry tends to treat information as proprietary. We don't work together.

Many problems can be traced to lack of communication. Manufacturers don't seem to be producing what consumers want to buy but rather what they think the market wants. They produce furniture that doesn't meet the taste, scale, or use demands of the market. They're not consulting designers or their clients. The "old boys" think they know the industry. They're not recognizing that there have been major changes and designers and clients now have different wants and needs. It is often difficult to find products that fit within the types of spaces found in the buildings of today. We work very hard to find just the right pieces and are often forced to pay very high prices in order to get exactly what a client needs.

Manufacturers have been reducing the prices of some furniture. It's amazing to see how the costs keep coming down due to imports. On the whole, according to the American Research Group, as stated in a recent publication of *Home Furnishings Daily*, consumers today expect a sofa to last only 8.3 years. With this lower-priced product, they feel very comfortable disposing of it and doing something new. This is so against all of our standards of sustainability.

Manufacturers in the contract industry began coordinating colors throughout diverse product lines a number of years ago. This shared information gave us laminates, metal finishes, carpets, and fabrics—a whole range of coordinated products. Not only does this save time for the designer and client but allows each product to help sell the next. In the residential field, it is often impossible to find a carpet or plain fabric that works with the new patterned fabrics. The patterns are freshly styled to fit today's market. The other items that are needed for the balance of the room are often unavailable until several years later. By that time, the designers have moved on to other products.

Manufacturers are hiring famous people from the fashion world, from Hollywood, and, in a few cases, even Donald Trump to "style" their lines. They are telling the public that these are the leaders who can show us how to live. This isn't always the right answer, because interior designers are exposed to the needs of clients on a regular basis. They understand clients' needs.

Another problem is that product testing is often done after the furniture and furnishings hit the market. Products are tested for safety and durability, but not for consumer acceptance. One appliance manufacturer spent more to test a new refrigerator than the entire furniture industry had spent on research in the previous decade. This has long been a complaint of furniture designers. The vast majority of manufacturers agree that consumer research can help the industry. One company that is taking the lead is Leggett and Platt, according to information distributed to clients and designers by the company.

Today, designers and clients are becoming part of the research and development teams of many leading corporations. Leggett and Platt just opened a large research center called the Idea Center. This facility is stocked with products, innovative computer systems, and testing equipment. Leggett and Platt has a system whereby both designers and clients can express their needs and wants. The system then links the desires of end users with the company's engineering department. With this ongoing interaction, Leggett and Platt is better able to find the right products for its clients.

But if, as pollsters claim, appearance is what drives the industry and what makes consumers buy, why should the industry spend money testing products?

We should test products because appearance includes perceived value. Consumers are very conscious of value and quality. Sometimes a manufacturer's perception of value and quality is very different from a client's. Every other product consumers can buy, from automobiles to toasters, has been tested extensively, and the manufacturers emphasize that fact in promotional materials. This is one area in which the home furnishings industry has some catching up to do. Fortunately, fabrics are now being extensively tested, especially for the contract field. We're seeing wear standards on most of our tags. This has helped a great deal. But, other than fabrics, many of our furniture pieces used in residential work have very few established standard measurements.

A proposal regarding the educational systems for designers suggested that design schools become research and testing centers for furniture. Students are intensely interested in construction and detail. They would be great critics and research reviewers for products.

AN INDUSTRY REPORT CARD

At several design workshops, I asked a group of designers, architects, and business managers to evaluate how well our resources met their needs and challenges. The categories considered were product quality and design, service, speed of production, technical information, and concern for the environment and environmental illness. Rarely did any participant give the industry a grade higher than a mediocre *C*. Our industry is expected to represent quality, service, and innovation!

There are so many areas that affect the end product, that each of these small issues requires exceptional control. If one little item breaks down we have a problem. That problem reflects back on the interior designer who specified the product.

Quality Control of Products

Overall, quality is improving, but we often feel it's not quite what it should be. Naturally, this depends on the type of product we're dealing with. Companies that work with the basics are often considered some of the best resources. The basics are certain types of furniture and styles of fabric that we use repeatedly because we know they work, such as a plain fabric or a simple, comfortable piece of furniture. Sometimes they're very difficult to find because they are so versatile and desirable.

Sometimes companies style items to an extreme. They make furniture that may be stylish but isn't comfortable. It just doesn't meet the basic needs of clients in specific situations. When we find a resource that pays attention to our requirements, smart designers make a point of saying that they will remember that resource and try their best to use their products often. This is why many of us are working hard to build our teams, not just of consultants, but of resources—so that we can deliver a quality job to our clients.

Speed of production is one area designers believe manufacturers in our country are doing well. However, products coming from other countries are often irregular and sporadic in their production due to a few different factors. If you're dealing with a fabric or something easy to ship quickly, the delivery is usually fantastic. But if a product requires custom care, these shipments are very erratic. It depends heavily on the management of the company. If the companies have invested in their own factories, and have total control of them worldwide, then conditions are much better. However, if a company is subcontracting the components of its products, this can create delay.

Recently, during a tour of the San Francisco Design Center, I discovered that almost every piece I liked and requested information on was made in the United States. This is a great change from a number of years ago, when most of the products we bought were made in other countries. Today, products from Europe are more expensive due to the exchange rate on the dollar. Today there's still an influx of inexpensive products coming from other countries, such as Asia or South America. However, American companies are taking advantage of the benefits of technology and high-quality equipment. They're able to do better, more exacting work with fewer people. But these people are more highly skilled and trained. American companies are also able to finish quality pieces and deliver them quickly, which is not possible when pieces have to travel from a distance.

Furniture moved from one climate to another can present a real problem. Wood grown in this country is often greatly superior. It's long-lived and far denser than wood from Asian countries.

In her article, "Furniture Experts Discuss Industry," Emma Burgin reiterated these points.[1] Manufacturing is returning to this country, and better quality products are being produced. Hickory Chair explained a few years ago that the majority of its larger pieces are made in America; only its small accessory pieces are imported. Century Chair is also bringing back the manufacturing of its major pieces. The company has found out that even though its costs were 40 percent less abroad than here, the products really didn't have the quality of craftsmanship and design it wanted. From 2000 to 2006, we saw many companies moving offshore and North Carolina lost 20 percent of its furniture manufacturing jobs, but companies and jobs are now returning. The fascinating thing is these companies aren't necessarily in formerly key manufacturing locations such as North Carolina, but all over the United States.

Impact on the Environment

In issues regarding environmental illnesses or problems, the industry is definitely improving, but the record is also pretty spotty. So often we know parts of the conditions of production and the sustainability issues, but something may be in the packing, finish, or shipping technique that may destroy the integrity of the product. We definitely need more information about this; our public and designers are demanding it. In the areas of concern for the environment and environmental illness, the group of designers in our Designers' Business Forum gave the industry almost failing grades, but they do see improvement. Their comments included:

"We need more information on the levels of formaldehyde and other toxins in products."

"While fabrics are labeled for fiber content, there is no indication of which finishes are applied or if toxic chemical components exist."

New Product Development

In the first edition of his book *In Search of Excellence*, Tom J. Peters praised the design industry, citing Herman Miller as a positive example.[2] But in a later speech and book, Peters wrote that office furniture introductions were "boring, boring, boring!"—and the residential line is not much better. The furnishings and design industry is not providing the new-product excitement the consumer wants. Change stimulates people to invest money in their interior spaces. Some clients do want the latest fashion; others want products that improve the way they live and work.

In the apparel industry, a certain percentage of each line is designed for runway success only; its real purpose is to generate publicity that may cause buyers to rethink the line.[3] In our field we have fine art pieces that are usually made by smaller firms. It's always fun to visit ICFF, the International Contemporary Furniture Fair, each May in New York City. Artisans from all over the world present their latest products, which are inspiring to designers and consumers alike.

Manufacturers at our various markets present a lot of prototypes, especially since they're having them made in foreign places and have to order greater volumes. The manufacturers want to make sure these items will sell, so they often presell a substantial amount before they actually put them into production. This means when we see an item at market, it may be a year or longer before it's available to the trade. This can be very difficult, because, as designers, we often need the products for a project we are working on, and our clients aren't happy to wait.

One of the problems in the industry is that some companies make very formal furniture of wonderful quality, but people aren't living as formally as they did. For example, some companies still believe in a formal dining room, although many consumers today don't have one. Our clients want good furniture and are willing to pay the price, but they want more casual finishes or less formal designs. Tradition is restricting some companies from moving into markets in which quality furniture is needed and appreciated.

Michael K. Dugan, chairman and CEO of Henredon Furniture Industries, has another view about what's wrong with our industry. Dugan says, "I think one of the most atrocious mistakes we have made is to allow our thinking to lean to the conclusion that 'If it's ugly, it will sell; if it's good looking, it won't sell.' Good design is salable."[4]

Most designers find that their clients want good design and things that work. They want pieces that fit their lifestyles. Often furniture doesn't sell, not because it's "ugly" or "good looking" but because it just doesn't work in the types of homes we have today.

There's also an issue of scale. Today we have very large homes or very small ones. We really need different scales of furniture. It's difficult when looking in a catalog to determine the scale of a particular piece of furniture. The pieces may be shown in equal ways, which can be very confusing, even to the professional.

The furniture industry has been borrowing from the apparel industry since the late 1970s, with an influx of couture designers that began when Terence Conran opened his first store in the United States. Furniture and home furnishings manufacturers became licensees for designers such as Pierre Cardin and Oleg Cassini. In 1999 we saw Ralph Lauren and Laura Ashley get into the picture. Since then, there have been many more, such as Nicole Miller, Armani, Missoni, Versace, and Fendi. At a recent High Point Market, there was a tremendous display of Donald Trump designs.

There are also interior designers such as Barbara Barry, Laura Kirar, Thomas Pheasant, Jacques Garcia, and Bill Sofield, who have either an industrial or interior design background but are also involved in designing furniture pieces and seem to be doing very well. Designers coming from the fashion field usually have industrial designers or furniture designers who assist by doing the technical work on their designs.

Pricing Issues

Pricing is often an issue, since everyone is wondering what price sheets mean. It's so confusing when we see three and four "retail" or "list" price lists from one manufacturer and then find that large contracts are awarded at 81 percent off-list. The professionals in the field can't help but wonder, what is retail or list price? If it's confusing to the designer and field professionals, we know how extremely confusing it must be to our clients. This is also very destructive. It undermines the integrity and credibility of the field and raises a lot of deserving questions that are hard to answer.

Quality Control

Our industry is introducing many new products, some at one-tenth the price of standard items that have been copied in a Third World country. It's so unfortunate to realize that much of the quality is not there, even though at first glance the product appears to have a similar design. It's disturbing to see good designs self-destruct because of improper construction. "Every business day sees too many new interior design products coming to market with little to commend except low cost," writes Roger Yee, former editor of *Contract Design* magazine.[5]

DISTRIBUTION PROBLEMS

American-made furniture has benefited from modern technology, which permits manufacturers to produce a better product at less cost. However, the imports are being made much less expensively than anything domestic. We have an additional problem, which is today's distribution. We now see upholstered furniture being made in China, but we're also told it costs $180 in freight to bring a sofa from China into our country. This means that even very inexpensive furniture can become more expensive. Since these items are mass-produced, there isn't flexibility in color or design. At present, you are going to have to buy it as it comes.

Transportation is also extremely expensive. You used to be able to figure that it cost you $30 to $40 to receive a chair. Now, sometimes the freight alone can run up into the hundreds, depending on which part of the country the furniture item comes from. This is always an issue when you select different vendors. Nowadays one needs to consider the cost of shipping—as well as the condition of the piece of furniture upon arrival. It's sad to see furniture leaving the factory in beautiful condition and arriving in an unusable condition.

Today distribution can be as much as 85 percent of a product's price. Distribution is defined as every cost—administrative, selling, showroom expenses, taxes, and insurance—except the cost of materials and labor. The future of interior design and furnishings will be based not only on making quality products at a lower cost but also on finding a better and less expensive method of distribution.

We've lost our traditional distribution structures. At one time it was furniture in department stores. Today, fewer than 5 percent of the stores that were around twenty years ago remain. The number of office furniture dealers has also dwindled. There is a pent-up desire on the part of consumers for furniture and furnishings, but there are fewer places to see, test, and try out new items.

EDUCATING THE CONSUMER

Today you can buy food, clothing, or furniture quickly and easily. Stores such as Whole Foods show you what to do with the food you buy. Professionals explain the products in detail. This presentation has captured the attention of many consumers. The same is happening in the interior design field. Clients are looking for designers who really understand the detailing of products and are able to answer their questions. This demand is making a positive change on our industry.

The retail industry was traditionally dedicated to education as well as supply, and this dedication is seeing a rebirth today. Because we don't have as many traditional furniture stores anymore, customers are dependent on smaller stores or the design studios to explain the value and advantages of a particular product: how it works, how to use it, and how to maintain it. As customers learn about a product, they begin to need it and then want to buy it.

Clients are looking for more places where they can try products, which is why interior design studios are often adding a small showroom area where clients can test particular favorite chairs. We are also seeing large stores that are destination sites, which clients visit just for the purposes of having a chance to sit in furniture they have perhaps seen in magazines or catalogs. They really want to try some of the pieces before purchasing them.

Furniture has become much more expensive, and people are realizing they have wasted a lot of money just to stock yard sales on their front lawns. This was not the way we bought many years ago. Whether it was clothing or furnishings, we bought things to last. We also expected an educated salesperson and extensive service. Retail stores had long-term employees who knew their customers. In traditional furniture stores and design studios, the interior designer helped you select furniture that worked together. It didn't matter that it might take years to finish the home. If you had a problem with a product even eight years after you bought it, there was a system to take care of your problem.

Because many products are mass produced and, therefore, much less expensive today, products that a few years ago were available only through interior designers or qualified dealers are in the general market at less cost than we could buy them. This gives the consumer the illusion that designers are no longer needed. With the lower prices, consumers feel they can afford to make a mistake. The disparity in pricing lends the impression that price is the main issue in whether or not to buy. The industry must refocus the consumer's attention on other factors.

Enhancing the Consumer's Experience

Consumers may be able to buy many new products, but they don't understand how to use them. As a result, products are often being used incorrectly. This diminishes the value of the products and can poison a consumer's perception of the manufacturer. Consumers are losing the opportunity to live with and enjoy many of the products the furnishing and design industry can offer.

Industry surveys today tell us that customers want information and the return of the knowledgeable salesperson or designer. Experience supports that belief. There's an unlimited demand for products and design services. We have all designed rooms for ourselves which we thought were great until the next furniture market, where we saw a new product that fit even better into our present way of life or had better quality. Once a client has a chair that really fits and is made of quality materials, he or she wants that particular product—not the older, lower-quality item. Clients have learned that there is a difference.

People need to experience design products. Electronic retailing has become strong in the home furnishings industry. The Internet is a great place to do research and to comparison shop, but it's not enough. It doesn't let you touch a fabric or really walk through a space. Department and furniture stores used to let you walk in and feel you had entered a room in a home. They displayed beautiful examples, such as setups of full kitchens with people cooking in them. But these types of department and furniture stores are decreasing.

To sell design products, we need to present them well. Catalogs, television, and computer screens aren't enough because they don't provide enough of the tactile and experiential aspects. They don't give you the opportunity to actually sit on a chair.

Furniture, fabrics, carpets, and accessories must be touched, felt, sat in, and experienced. Seeing a picture of a room and actually being in it are quite different experiences. Walt Disney said we must deal with all the senses. Interior design incorporates and appeals to all of them. Our challenge is to educate through real experiences.

Specialists have taken the lead in creating a total experience. Kitchen specialists have kitchens you walk into and see the products being used. They bring in a chef to show you how to use the appliances. You can eat a meal the chef has prepared, tasting the results. Bed and bath shops are now featuring everything from plumbing fixtures to towels and soap. You have the opportunity to sit in the tub and try different components to see what really fits you. It's always amazing when I take people to try different fixtures and see how they respond to the experience. It's obvious that different shapes and sizes of products are made for the different shapes and sizes of people. We've learned that experiences are what people want. Whether that experience be in entertainment or interior design, they want to see, taste, and feel. This is necessary for our kind of products.

We are seeing more and more of these experiences, from home expos to fine specialty shops, popping up everywhere for people to see and use products. Some of these centers also have experts who come with them, but others do not. The expert is an important component because clients want to know what works and what doesn't. They need the personal input only a professional can give them.

WHAT BUSINESS ARE WE IN?

The industry is attacking the distribution problem on several fronts. Design centers, traditionally geared only to people in the trade, have begun to open their doors to the public. This alienates interior designers and architects who see open centers as direct competition.

Design centers and their tenants must decide what business they're in: wholesale or retail. Tenants of design centers are in the business of selling wholesale. They're used to conveying information at the designer level, generally more complex than that of the consumer.

Designers are taught to take responsibility for the major part of a job. They're looking for particular details, rather then having someone help them coordinate a space. This is quite different from someone servicing retail.

With wholesale, it's understood that another person or group will handle the direct retail education and customer service. The retailer handles service and communication with the end user, including everything from the presentation of products to clients in their own language (as opposed to designer language), to the delivery and the manner in which it is executed, to the repairs and problem solving for the next few years.

Many products in design centers are created for experienced designers. They're not easy to use; they're special and unusual. Putting home furnishings and design products in the wrong places, using them incorrectly, or representing them as doing things they will not do well is bad for both the manufacturer and the designer. If a very delicate chair is placed where it gets heavy use, it will be destroyed. Using good products inappropriately hurts the entire design industry.

Someone has to make the judgment of what belongs where. This is the traditional role of the designer and this responsibility should rest with the designer. Designers have both the scientific and the artistic backgrounds to judge where a piece should or should not be used. When design centers sell directly to the public, who makes that judgment? Selling directly to consumers entails the responsibilities of visiting the location, as designers do; observing the ways people use furniture; and passing judgment about the correct application of products.

When a product is delivered and needs repair, who takes care of it? For design centers to deal responsibly with consumers, they need service departments—facilities that follow through on and maintain the furnishings they sell.

Many design centers have invested extensively in developing a building to communicate the design experience. That's great! It's part of future consumer education. However, a building is not enough. Design centers that sell directly to the consumer are doing themselves and the manufacturers a disservice. Manufacturers and designers both need to understand that full service should be available. Buying furniture without a specification is like buying medicine without a prescription. Consumers realize they're buying furniture without a safety net but see no alternative.

MARKETS AND CONFERENCES

Industry trade shows and conferences are very important to interior designers. There are many of them—local, national, and international. In fact, markets are becoming increasingly important because there aren't as many showroom resources as there used to be. Many companies find markets are their only way of presenting their products to designers. Designers are now spending much more time at these markets. For example, many designers spend as much as a week or more at the High Point Market, finding their time there to be well spent. They can review and compare a wide range of products they may want to use in their projects.

The home furnishings market has created a new service called Market Scout. The program was created by Dr. Richard B. Bennington, chair of High Point University. Market scouts are design students familiar with the general vocabulary of the field as well as the market itself. A designer may request information about a product, such as the price range, style, and general conditions from a market scout. These researchers investigate products for designers and put together an agenda, which is then sent to the designer for approval. At the scheduled date of arrival, the scout meets the designer to escort him or her through selected showrooms. This service allows designers to learn of new product sources and also saves them time.

I was really impressed to see the diversity of people at High Point Market. There are dealers and designers from all parts of the country and the world. Some seem to be very prosperous, arriving in magnificent vehicles and impeccably dressed. Then there are the more conservative people, who appear to be coming from smaller communities and who have driven halfway across the country in modest vehicles. But all are looking forward to the new products, something that will bring excitement and interest to their companies. They have great hope to find resources that can help them secure a profitable income during the coming year. It's a wonderful experience to see so many people you know and to share experiences of the past year. Seeing the many thousands of design professionals together at a market like this is an overwhelming experience.

Brian Casey, president and CEO of the High Point Market Authority, was asked in an interview how important interior designers are to the market. He said, very important. Casey pointed out that interior designers come to the market for many different reasons. First, they come to see the trends and new products, whether in their own markets or elsewhere. These designers may have a particular specialty, but they want to be aware of what's happening in other specialties as well. He said designers also come to find better options for their clients. They realize there are resources at the High Point Market that extend beyond what they can see in other markets. There are opportunities to purchase better products at more reasonable prices.

Casey pointed out that the Market hires interior designers to work on its pressrooms. For example, because the Market didn't have a budget to completely redo its space architecturally, the staff hired an interior designer to update the existing space. The changes were a pleasant surprise to all—they showed the Market really cares about the professionals who attend. Casey also pointed out that much resourcing is being done online. Interior designers often reference companies via the Internet, which they have been introduced to through the Market over the years.

Reaching Out

Design centers have instituted various programs to introduce potential clients to designers. For example, Designer Days is a program in which potential clients can "Meet the Designer" at the New York Design Center, located at 200 Lexington Avenue. They have designers working for them who are ready to be of service to a client who wants to purchase only a few pieces. Or, these designers may introduce the client to a designer ready to take on a much larger project. But there's still a lot of confusion about how we handle the clients of designers versus the consumer who just wants to buy.

Traditionally, design centers were only for wholesale—in this case to furniture stores or interior designers. The Lexington Design Center is one example. Now, almost all design centers serve the retail client. The questions a designer has are very likely to be different from those of an average consumer. Therefore, these centers have difficulty finding appropriate staffing. If it's wholesale, a center needs to be staffed with people of great knowledge who can answer designers' questions. If it's a retail center, the process is much different.

Commercial design has undergone many changes. Today, most of the larger office or commercial projects are done by interior designers. They're the ones who arrange the connections and the purchasing—sometimes directly through factories and sometimes through very large dealerships—often from a distance. There are fewer typical "office furnishings" companies than there were, but there are major resources servicing the commercial or office business clients with excellence.

Christopher Kennedy is executive vice president of Merchandise Mart Properties, which owns and manages the Merchandise Mart in Chicago, numerous buildings at High Point, and design centers throughout the country.[6] Kennedy says the answer lies in viewing the consumer, rather than architects and designers, as the ultimate client in the distribution channel. This means strengthening the position of designers and architects as non-stocking dealers to replace diminishing retail sources.

Distribution is a challenge: delivering the right product in the right manner to the right people at the right price. Clients relate to the designer, and the designer recommends and specifies products. We need a smooth process of distribution, because the process reflects on the designer.

Notes

1. Emma Burgin. "Furniture Experts Discuss Industry," *High Point Enterprise*, February 2, 2007.
2. Thomas J. Peters. *In Search of Excellence: Lessons from America's Best-Run Companies.* New York: HarperCollins, 2004.
3. Mark McIntyre. "Selling Innovative Design," *Interior Design*, January 1991, p. 42.
4. Harvey Probber. "Executive Involvement in the Design Process," *Interior Design*, May 1990, pp. 62–64.
5. Roger Yee. "It's Cheap—and It's No Good!" *Contract Design*, May 1994, p. 8.
6. Kristen Richards. "Design Centers: Public or Private?" *Interiors*, April 1994, pp. 30–36.

CHAPTER 5

TRENDS AND THE MARKET

Running a design business today without tracking the trends is like designing a home for a person you've never met and know nothing about. It's possible, but it's a lot harder than it has to be.

Being a news junkie or reading four newspapers a day doesn't guarantee you'll be aware of all the events that affect the design industry. You can't rely on the late-night news to tell you everything you need to know. You have to combine knowledge of client demands and industry involvement. A pioneer trend-tracker and author of *Trend Tracking*, Gerald Celente suggests that if you read only one newspaper a week, read Saturday's.[1] It has the most vital information relating to business. Saturday's paper is smaller and will feature weekend statements about business. Because Saturday's news is read after the stock market closes, businesses time any press releases about negative changes or losses for the weekend in the hope that the news will be "old" by Monday and will no longer have an impact when the market re-opens. Newspapers also often run articles on trends in weekend editions.

SPOTTING A TREND

A trend is a predictable sequence of events. "You need at least two points to plot a direction," says Celente. "At first you won't know if what you're seeing is a trend or not." A trend also must have social, economic, and political significance. If the effects are trivial, or the events have only political importance, they're not a trend.

Trend watchers such as Celente and Ken Dychtwald, president of Age Wave Inc., suggest you keep trend files with very broad categories. *Home Office Computing* magazine gives homelessness as an example of one of the fastest-growing trends. The magazine places homelessness in the category of "family," which has effects on politics, health, and the economy. The key to a good trend-tracking system is recognizing connections between fields.

Trend tracking is something you'll have to do for yourself, Celente cautions. Having someone else do it is like having someone else exercise for you.

Finally, maintain a sense of proportion, and don't get too far ahead of your market because, as Dychtwald says, "You can't make money as an entrepreneur twenty years ahead. You have to be two years ahead."[2]

When CAD came in, we all saw it as having a future. But it took a long time until CAD was affordable for the average practice. For a company to invest $300,000 to $400,000 on elaborate CAD equipment was hard to rationalize; it wasn't cost-effective for most firms. Ken Dychtwald says you can't make money as an entrepreneur twenty years ahead of time because people aren't ready for the market. For example, when fax machines came out, we were one of the first firms to buy one, but we didn't have anyone to fax things to. Equipment has come down in price so considerably that almost everyone can afford it. This is true of technology in general.

In the 1970s, when Saphier Lerner Schindler became SLS Environetics and developed computer programs that enabled its architects and designers to design on a mainframe computer, individual designers regarded this computer as a tool for gargantuan design firms. Today CAD work can even be done on a laptop.

SLS Environetics invested in its future, predicted a need, and probably created a demand. Initially, the learning curve was so steep that it took two years for the firm to train its own architects to use the tool. Principals predicted that someday every designer would use computers as a design tool. A lot of us thought they were dreaming and that they were just like off-the-wall futurists who, in the early 1970s, predicted paperless offices.

Manufacturers of residential furniture targeted the home office in the late 1980s, producing office furnishings to complement various home decors. Interior designers and contract furniture manufacturers didn't take the trend seriously enough. Some office dealers did, but their requests for a quick-delivery, low-cost line were ignored. Today, large office supply companies have extensive collections of furnishings in stock, ready for immediate delivery.

Other Trends

- Appearance, not construction, drives the furniture industry.
  Source: America's Research Group
- Small businesses that employ fewer than one hundred people are creating jobs faster than larger businesses.
  Source: Rukeyser
- Word-of-mouth accounts for at least 67 percent of designer referrals.
  Source: America's Research Group
- The U.S. retail e-commerce sales for the first quarter of 2006 was $25.2 billion, an increase of 7.0 percent from the fourth quarter of 2005.
  Source: The Census Bureau of the Department of Congress

TRENDS IN THE TWENTY-FIRST CENTURY

Now, in the twenty-first century, designers must find a way to differentiate themselves from the pack. As Seth Godin wrote in his book, *Purple Cow*, designers must do something that stands out.[3] The Web today is the great equalizer. Everyone has access to the same resources and information. Customers have the power. They know how to get the information once only accessible to professionals. They have Web sites, e-mail contacts, and chat rooms where they can get extensive product information. They often know more than we do about products and about our resources that they would have never known before.

Today our clients are exposed to many products. If they don't see a difference between them, they'll buy the least expensive one. We need to show them that it's worth it to invest in better products. Once they realize this, they often want nothing but the best. Another twenty-first century change is that there's much less respect for longevity and experience. People don't care how long you've been in business. They just care what you're doing today and what you're giving them that someone else can't.

Things That Aren't Working

Cost cutting isn't as effective now as it was previously. Companies once sought cheap labor and inexpensive suppliers. However, the bargain hunting strategy only weakened those that employed it. Today, strong companies have dedicated staff they pay well. They are buying much better products to ensure their end results are of a quality they want to stake their reputations on. Sales or reduced prices have hurt almost every field. Why should we train clients to look for bargains? We need to teach them that ours is a credible field that gives them good products for appropriate prices.

Small improvements are not of interest to clients today. Improving a hinge or a little detail doesn't cut it. Clients want something new and exciting.

Advertising and marketing are very expensive and aren't as effective as they once were. The only exception is if you have something really great and worth talking about. Then it's worth investing in advertising and marketing.

Expanding a company by literally making it larger often proves very destructive. It requires such a complex management structure that leaders of the company are often placed in positions of management when they really should be dealing with clients or production.

Following the needs of clients isn't enough. We must direct their needs and show clients where they need to be going. We must help create a future for them and show them how things can be done better. An example of a company that does a great job of serving client needs is the Progressive Group of Insurance Companies. The company brings an adjuster right to an accident site, often within an hour of the time it was reported. The adjuster files the claim and writes the check immediately, right on the spot. The client is told that if there is a problem, the adjuster will be happy to correct it later. Instead of putting the client through an ordeal involving extensive office work, details, and papers, the company uses available technology to expedite the process. Clients can move on to get their repairs taken care of immediately. This is a system worth emulating. The fewer people involved, the faster and more efficiently a process can be done. Plus, it builds rapport with clients.

Following fads doesn't work, either. By the time we start putting a fad into place, it's gone and out of style. We need to look for items that have meaning, or they're not worth the investment.

We all write letters of agreement, contracts, and other basic documents to protect ourselves legally. Designer associations actively help us understand the issues of liability. But the most important way to prevent legal problems is to do excellent work. If we put our emphasis on doing wonderful work and staying close to our clients, it's amazing how many legal issues can be prevented. We can't just rely on contracts and legal protections. We really need to put every effort into making sure everything we do is the very best it can be.

RECOGNIZING A PATTERN

How do you recognize an event of global importance—one that will have an impact on you and your business? It's not always readily apparent. Operation Desert Storm showed us that the age of high technology was not on the way, but was already here. The war was fought with computers. Computers, modems, and satellite receivers mean easy access to knowledge. War wasn't the dynamic change. It was the graphic demonstration of the power rapid communications brings to a venture. Since the early nineties, computers have become an indispensable part of our world. They're part of our lives in every aspect of work and communication. We must accommodate computers in every space we design. They have changed our services, as well. It may be hard to sell space planning since Steelcase and other major suppliers will send CAD-drawn plans in twenty-four hours with a suggested furniture plan.

Technology

As previously discussed, technology has changed the way we work and think. It has taken over a lot of the repetitive work that absorbed so much office time. It has even caused spelling changes. The Spanish language has eliminated two letters from its alphabet to become more computer-friendly.

Technology has altered our lives in yet another profound way: it has changed our perception of history. Modern technology is proving many "facts" to be incorrect. For example, paint chips and wallpaper scraps from historic houses have been digitally analyzed, giving us a truer picture of the colors used in those eras. You can no longer rely solely on your favorite old design books, like those by Wallace Nutting and Sherrill Whiton, who wrote the bibles of our industry.

In addition to rewriting history, technology adds information. A hundred people of different sizes and occupations sat on electronic sensor mats to measure how weight is distributed across a Knoll's Parachute Chair's seat and back.[4] The pressure "maps" were used to shape the chair and adjust its foam to reduce pressure hot spots.

Through technology, we are bringing expert information and materials to our clients and staffs for every portion of our projects—from selling to the smallest detail.

Green Issues

Designer publications and markets all emphasize green issues. As this area develops further, there will be more scrutiny over everything we put into a space. We've been concerned about commercial buildings, but we need to be just as concerned with what goes into a residence. People are being poisoned in so many ways. Just to cite one example, we've seen it happening in food with the many recalls that have taken place in the past few years. What will be next? We think things are safe, but we're unsure and our industry is no exception. We're going to be seeing more of these green issues coming to the forefront in our business.

Our insurance policies are now excluding anything related to mold. Mold has been an issue in buildings for many years. All of a sudden, it's the new radon. This adds a new factor to the interior design mix. We have to deal with visible and invisible issues. An environment should function well for its inhabitants. It should look good, and if it doesn't actively support good health, it certainly shouldn't poison the people who live in it. It's no longer enough to have a general understanding of how furniture is constructed. We also have to know which components of the things we buy are likely to cause health issues and their relation to other problems, such as flammability, when they come into contact with common substances. Formaldehyde, for example, is one of the common substances that can be found in furniture that people shouldn't be exposed to for very long.

Air quality is a consciousness-raising issue. It put a hotel in Philadelphia out of business due to an airborne bacterium now called *Legionella*. Concern for air quality has led to laws on public smoking. Sick-building syndrome puts every product that goes into a building under scrutiny—from the adhesives used to lay carpets to the fabric finishes, from the composition of furniture and paints to maintenance products. The main worry is no longer whether furniture produces toxic gases in a fire, but what common products contaminate our air. I cannot help but wonder how many currently standard items will someday be proven sources of serious contaminants. As designers, we have used many of them. You can bet we will be held responsible for their effects.

We don't immediately know when a specific event will kick-start a dynamic change that affects the way we do business. A blaring headline or a long story on the nightly news doesn't necessarily indicate this. It may take a month or two to build significance, or it may take several years. An event that was a throwaway news item at first could turn out to be the starting point for a world-shaking change. You'd never know it unless you had a basis for comparison. That's why you can't read one newspaper a month and listen half-heartedly to the nightly news, then expect to be well-informed. Some design firms join groups such as our Designers' Business Forum or hire consultants to keep them apprised of these different issues.

Small is Beautiful

Hammer and Champy's *Reengineering the Corporation*, mentioned earlier, talked about the mergers and changes of companies. But the book didn't spark the trend. It only reported and advised readers on how to manage the change.

We in the interior design industry knew before other industries that a company can get only so big before the system starts working against it. Quick changes become impossible.

We saw in the last quarter of the twentieth century that large companies such as Burlington bought Stendig, and Dolly Madison Ice Cream bought several furniture companies. Many other large conglomerates were created and Furniture Brands International bought a dozen or more smaller furniture companies.

There are so many changes that have affected our industry that it's difficult to name all of them.

- The computer and the Internet have had a dramatic impact on everything. We thought at one time the computer was just a communication tool. We now realize it's part of every industry and every aspect of our lives.
- CAD is part of all our studios. My studio employed designers who were great at drafting. They could draft manually just as fast as someone on CAD. Now that we're e-mailing everything, it *must* be done on CAD. That way we're able to send our information anywhere in the world with great ease, efficiency, and accuracy. There's no question CAD has changed our whole perspective—from the smallest detail of our work to extremely large design projects.
- Corporations are constantly changing. One is buying another, they're revamping, etcetera. We often see these changes being made on a dime. It doesn't take a lot of study or review. From the perspective of interior designers, we see these changes happening overnight and impacting the whole industry. This is evident in the companies we purchase from. We place an order today with one company and, in a few months, when we go to place a second order with that same company, it's under a completely different name with a different administrative body and buying structure. We're also seeing large companies that were no longer as productive being bought by experienced staff members and then becoming very successful. Now the newly formed companies are on a more appropriate scale and can serve designers' particular needs.
- Instead of companies wanting to be large, they're acting like small companies by emphasizing personal relationships. Eye contact is still the most important form of

communication in a relationship. As much as we love all forms of technology, there's nothing more valuable than the time we spend across the table with someone reviewing a situation. We use all the other support systems of communication, but those personal relationships are becoming more important than ever.

- Virtual companies, or companies made up of different components all over the world, are part of the norm today. We no longer look just to our staff for expertise; we realize we have the knowledge and skill of many specialists throughout the world, which we can pull from on a regular basis.

Large corporations were unsuccessful in operating furniture factories because they thought these companies were just like their other assets. Furniture making requires craftsmanship and attention to fine details. It takes management that understands and appreciates the requests of the industry to run a productive company.

Today there's a growth in small firms that supply specialty items. This growth was in part an answer to the backlash against mass production—a backlash John Naisbitt termed "high touch." At the International Contemporary Furniture Fair in Javits Center, hundreds of craftspeople present their products. Now we see many of them represented by a marketing company because these craftspeople have realized that they don't have time to produce as well as go out and sell. They're finding companies who are masters in the sales arena to do it for them.

Changes in Mass Production

Another trend is that mass-produced products are being manufactured offshore in great volumes and at low prices. At the same time, we see more American-made merchandise and higher-quality products. Craftspeople who started in an academic environment and then moved on to serve apprenticeships with master craftsmen are now establishing small companies. Or they're merging into other companies, where they can bring their skills to produce some incredible products. Many craftspeople, because of their backgrounds and exposure, have a sensitivity for design. They're either designing themselves or hiring designers who understand the quality-interior market.

The United States now has high-tech machinery computer programmed and able to produce high-quality merchandise. Textiles in a wide variety of colors are being produced on these machines. Fabrics that could be made only on very expensive handlooms and in limited quantities are now available at more reasonable prices. We're finding beautiful merchandise with quality beyond anything we imagined before. These products are being produced in our country as well as offshore.

Lifestyle Changes

Another trend is that people are looking at lifestyle rather than career. In the 1950s, Dad could give his all to his business and the family would survive because Mom took care of the practicalities of life. In the 1970s, women tried to "have it all" by working at careers rather than jobs and then coming home to another full day's work maintaining their homes. Today women realize "having it all" isn't possible if you have to do it all yourself. Professionals often have to choose between dedicating some of their energies and years to child-rearing, or arranging systems through which child-rearing and home responsibilities are handled by others.

Today it's acceptable for men to play very strong, even dominant, roles in raising children. It's acceptable for women to choose to be mothers only, professionals only, or both. Some men have discovered satisfaction in sharing the chores of nurturing, cooking, and housekeeping. Not only that, but the physical aspects of housekeeping are a natural antidote to the stresses of the workplace. It turns out that the work you do at home can complement the work you do at work. Many people have taken their offices home so they can be part of their families' lives. They've arranged their schedules so that they participate in their children's activities. In some cases, these individuals may be caring for older parents. They've found a way to work at a high level but also maintain their personal lifestyle. We've also seen people moving to what in the past would have been considered vacation areas, so their lives can incorporate some of the pleasures of these beautiful environments.

There's been a change in values. It's no longer enough to have a great career. It has to be balanced by health-related personal enrichment and family life. Businesses have discovered that where this balance exists, fewer employees are forced to take advantage of corporate mental health and addiction programs.

There's also been a grassroots change in lifestyles, indicating a move toward group living: two or more families or single parents share living quarters, generally a house. They also share housekeeping and nurturing responsibilities. In Mendocino County, California, a group of friends built a compound currently used as a shared vacation space but designed with retirement and senior living in mind. Designing this type of community is very different from designing spaces for retirees. This type of living center offers a lot of productive activity and, therefore, requires different building structures and interior design.

Many young people have very large salaries and major bonuses. They're able to buy houses, luxury automobiles—everything that older people worked years to earn. It's incredible to see how young people are earning and spending their money. Young people are also being subsidized by parents so that they have what were considered the luxuries of life very early on. This is what they've been used to. These are their demands.

Another trend is a return to working at home. Many people who were forced out of or elected to leave staff positions now work as independent contractors. Some jobs are arranged so the employee spends only three days a week in the office, working from home the other two days.

Some retirees don't stop working completely. Many start new businesses or remain in the workforce as independent contractors and consultants, both paid and as volunteers.

People are working out of their homes, but many choose to go to an organized business space where they have interaction with other people in their discipline. They feel this gives them a definite division between home and work life.

There is now a choice. People are making a decision to work on a part-time, full-time, or shared-job basis.

Technology and a change in business attitudes have made working at home possible. It is a cottage industry, but with a difference.

Financial Conditions Affecting Our Market

We constantly see reports about housing referring to national averages. This really has no meaning for our local markets. What matters is what's happening in your particular locale. A trend can be very strong in Florida but weak in the West. Be very careful with how you use what you read because on the whole national averages don't affect our individual markets. What does affect them are consumer confidence, job security, and local opportunities.

At one point, a large percentage of our business resulted from people moving. Today, that number is only 20 percent. The other 80 percent is generated by people who have been in their homes a long time. Consumers are concerned about the value of their largest asset, which is often their home. They're also concerned about adjustable rates on their mortgages and the amount of their home equity. These concerns are always governed by the local housing market.

Financing

Because furniture was the second largest expense in which people invested, companies often needed to provide financing. In many cases, this provided a great source of income for the furniture companies. Today, there's less need for such financing. People can borrow money much less expensively with home equity loans. Or they may already have an arrangement for borrowing they prefer to use.

NOT THE TREND, THE REACTION

So much of our thinking is manipulated by futurists and supposed prophets who have the ear of the media. I was in attendance when a representative of the Club of Rome spoke at NeoCon in the early 1970s, predicting that in forty years, the world's supply of oil would be depleted. In 1973 and 1977 we had oil shortages and long lines at service stations.

It's forty years later. According to the Club of Rome's timetable, which was based on the technology of the time, we should have no oil left. But today there are more than ninety years of oil left to supply our country alone. The prediction of the 1970s was based on what was then current technology and standards. Drilling techniques have improved, oil wells are dug deeper, and the oil in Alaska has become accessible through the Alaskan Pipeline. Oil resources have been found in the ocean and many other parts of the world. Gasoline use is being reduced considerably. We're looking at buildings that will be considered ZEBs (Zero Energy Buildings) in the not-so-distant future. We may not need the quantity of oil we once thought we did.

I'm sure the Club of Rome's prediction was an overstatement, using predictions of disaster as a reason for change. Predicting disaster, if it leads to change, is more constructive than panicked rationing of resources in the event of actual disaster. As it turns out, we are finding ways of using less oil.

Throughout history there have been fears of shortages. In the 1800s, fear of a whale oil shortage caused international panic because everyone was afraid they would have no oil for their lanterns. But in 1859, fossil oil was discovered in Pennsylvania and served as a perfectly legitimate replacement. Before that, the British government thought England would be finished by the end of the 1800s because the country would run out of coal. By the end of the 1800s, Britain was using fossil oil and no disaster occurred.

The world economic system affects the interior furnishings industry. For example, silk was once very expensive, but changes in the world market have brought the price down. At one time, our studio had a silk rug worth $85,000. Ten years later the same rug was worth about $35,000. The rug had not changed; the difference was that China opened its market, and now we have a lot of silk. Whether they are silk carpets or clothing, we are buying silk products for a lot less money than ever before.

The world is full of resources, whether we use them or not. Technology and politics help determine availability. Russia has more raw materials than any other country in the world, but until recently it did not have the technology and was therefore unable to use what it had. At one time, most of the products in the furnishings field were very expensive to produce; there was a standard cost based on retail. Today, cost varies so much. Shipping may be far in excess of the actual cost of production, depending on where in the world a furnishing is being produced. There's such a wide set of variables that some items that were standard are no longer considered so.

In the movie *The Graduate* (1967), Dustin Hoffman's character asks his father's friend what he should do to be successful. Plastics, he was told. It was a joke, but actually, we can't imagine life without plastics. It's hard to say what a young person should go into today because things are changing so quickly. We have a whole different repertoire of products available in our market today.

How many items have you bought in the past year for your own use that existed twenty years ago? Not many. In the furnishings and design industry, there are wonderful products our clients don't know they need or don't know how to ask for because they don't know such products exist. We need to do something about this.

THE LIBRARY AND BEYOND

Libraries are as good as the materials they contain. Traditional libraries had stockpiles of sample books and dog-eared catalogs. We still have many of the catalogs and material samples we love because we enjoy having actual samples available to touch. However, the Internet is our great resource for everything from the news and newest trends to researching items and checking stock, finishes, or any of the fine details of a piece. The Internet gives us expert information we can then transform into a beautiful presentation for our clients.

Many companies no longer create actual catalogs; they're relying solely on the Internet for their cataloging. Smaller companies are using this virtual system because it's far less expensive than distributing paper catalogs. Many Internet sources are restricted. As professional designers, we must be very careful what our clients have access to, so we can be sure if we present a product as unique, it truly is. We've also found a lot of the information on the Internet is not accurate. Information needs to be carefully reviewed before putting it into our design project.

Architectural standards and all forms of specification are now available on CDs. The formats of these CDs are designed so that they can be merged with our specification package efficiently. Industry-specific software is available at a reasonable cost. At one time, it was extremely expensive. This software can often be tailored to fit your specific design firm's needs.

Our resources have been invested in proprietary software designed to work with CAD and other programs. In both the planning and programming stages of projects, beautiful renderings can be digitally developed using this software. From office furniture to kitchen cabinets, manufacturers have programs that help us present detailed renderings in a very short time. Previously these renderings might have taken days. They are also accurate and can be altered very easily when necessary.

Virtual reality, or interactive computer simulation, allows designers and clients to "walk" through and understand a space with greater ease. Virtual reality also provides a system for checking certain issues of concern; for example, it can test light flow, which would be very difficult to test without actually building a sample. Full-scale CAD drawings are often developed for special furniture so the designer, client, and manufacturer can see all the fine details of a piece before they begin production. These drawings are entered into the computer program where the designs are prepared for production with the exact details the designers have specified. We see more and more opportunities to produce new designs.

Virtual reality has become part of the way we think and work because we are constantly using computers in our work. This trains us to become computer savvy and to anticipate the differences between a computer-generated sample and its physical manifestation. There often is a synergy of these two experiences, virtual and real.

When the automobile was first invented, people said, We move by walking! How are we going to deal with sitting in a vehicle that moves faster than horses? What will happen to us? Well, in the case of virtual reality, we don't have to do anything. It's here and we'll deal with it. As with cars, unless we crash, we'll adjust. Some people love virtual reality and actually perform better with it.

Business Tools

- Computer-Aided Design software such as AutoCAD from Autodesk permits the user to refine a design without redrawing it from scratch for each change.
- Paperless manufacturing products are designed on CAD, digitized, and sent to PCs and other terminals on the factory floor.
- Groupware is a class of products that exchanges information, combining e-mail, networking, and database technologies.
- Customer service is provided to meet customer needs. This is so important that large North American companies are investing in technology that puts data about each customer at a given company's fingertips.
- Servers are computers that store files and run applications for networks of PCs, or "clients." Servers have replaced mainframes.
- Networks: Networked PCs are linked by wires to hubs, which permit different kinds of computers to communicate and share data.
- Voice recognition software enables users to enter text and numbers into a computer without touching a keyboard.
- Tablet PCs are lightweight computers with touch screens for penned entries.
- Flash technology works through flash memory chips that slip into computer notebooks, personal digital assistants, and cameras.
- Advanced fiber optics is considered the foundation of the information superhighway. Fiber optic networks carry voice, data, and images without copper wire, which is how most phone systems are still connected.
- Wireless technology hot spots, or WiFi, allow users to access networks wirelessly.
- Videoconferencing allows participants to hear and see who they're talking to. Desktop videoconferencing also allows them to share data.
- Graphics technology includes cordless pens and tablets more sensitive than keyboard and mouse, giving artists greater control over the images they create.

- Software packages combine computer-rendering technology, accounting systems, and quoting solutions all in one.

Notes

1. Gerald Celente. *Trend Tracking.* New York: John Wiley, 1990, p. 13.
2. Ken Dychtwald. Quoted in Michael Maren, "Predict the Future and Profit," *Home Office Computing.* January 1994, p. 54–58.
3. Seth Godin. *Purple Cow.* New York: The Penguin Group, 2003.
4. "Form and Function," *Wall Street Journal,* May 2, 1994, p. B1.

CHAPTER 6

TODAY'S CLIENTS

The client of today is quite different from the client of the past. While some of today's clients have less discretionary income because of additional expenses and pressures, others have considerably more. It's amazing to see the increased number of millionaires.

There are clients who think a design is wonderful—as long as their ideas are incorporated. Designers can create working partnerships with clients by showing them how to carry out their ideas and improve their own designs.

In fact, some of our greatest competition today is not other designers, but clients who do projects themselves. Often individuals enjoy expressing their creativity, and this is one of the ways they have been empowered to do that. Television programs and other media have encouraged people to do creative work. When they're interested in doing a design project at a higher level, they come to an interior designer. They ask the designer to show them how to do a project that goes beyond the level they're able to accomplish on their own.

Then we have the other clients, often professionals, who are extremely overworked. In the past, these people worked forty to fifty hours a week; now they're working fifty, sixty, seventy hours a week or more. Many of these hours are accompanied by great amounts of effort and stress. They reach the point where they want some of the things that are important to them in life, including a comfortable, attractive environment. They want to make certain decisions, but they need someone to make those decisions easy for them because they don't have the energy, effort, or time to invest in their interior plans. Sometimes these kinds of clients will come to a designer and say, I'm really looking for a different experience in my work or home environment. I want you to create a new experience for me. Though the designer may have very little interaction with the client, he or she is totally responsible for creating this new environment.

Our society has measured achievement by consumption. Today, time is our most precious commodity. The people who purchase design services often have very little time, which is one reason they want our services.

DEMOGRAPHICS

The demographics of the people spending money on furnishings have changed considerably in the past twenty years. In 1985, the major consumers were between forty-five and fifty-four years of age. Today, they are much younger. According to *Home Furnishings Daily*, the thirty-five to forty-four-year-olds make up the largest group, followed by the twenty-five to thirty-four and fifty-five to sixty-four-year-olds. It's fascinating to see how many trends have changed during the past two decades, which means the major market is not necessarily the middle-aged market or the people with experience buying furniture. In so many cases, young people who are making their first investment in furnishings can easily afford the services of an interior designer. This means that the profession needs to consider what these younger people are interested in and how they buy. We also find people sixty-five and older making considerable investments in their furnishings, and they are doing so at twice the level they did twenty years ago. They're not necessarily saving money for their children; they're very willing to invest in something for their own lifestyle.

MARKETING TO GENERATIONS X AND Y

In her book, *Mind your X's and Y's: Satisfying the 10 Cravings of a New Generation of Consumers*, Lisa Johnson speaks about connecting with Generations X and Y.[1] They have incredible buying power and are very important to our industry. Johnson emphasizes several points relevant to these groups.

- Experience. These clients want to try new things, something that changes their routine. New experiences are extremely important to them and the way they relate to our industry.
- Transparency. Generation X ers and Y ers don't like anything that is slick, overpackaged, or fake. They want to deal only with companies that are comfortable with full disclosure. Accountability is important to them.
- Reinvention. The minute Generations X and Y have a new way, the old systems just disappear.
- Connection. These clients want to interact, make suggestions and be part of the design. They're interested in customization. They don't care if an item isn't perfect as long as it has a part of them built into it.

For most of us, basic items such as food and shelter, which took up much of the income of previous generations, cost a small fraction of what we earn. So much of the money people spend is on discretionary items. However, many clients feel they have accumulated too many things and, as a result, look to spend more on fewer items of higher quality. They want a beautiful life—things that enhance their personal lifestyle. Professional designers can be very supportive in assisting such clients. We can show them how to elevate their lifestyle and become very environmentally concerned. We can help them buy products that aren't wasteful and have great value and long-term use, so clients aren't replacing them so quickly. Clients who "did it themselves," and did a reasonably good job of it, are now looking to professionals to do something far beyond what they are capable of accomplishing on their own.

In 2005, there were 800,000 new millionaires in the United States, an increase of about 10 percent. Now there are a total of 8.3 million millionaires, one reason so many designers are concentrating their efforts on the luxury market. These very wealthy people often demand the best of what we have to offer, and there are many more of them out there.

CHANGED INCOMES

According the U.S. census, in 2005, 32.5 percent of all income in the U.S. was earned by households with earnings over $150,000, the top 5 percent. Approximately one fifth, or 20.58 percent, of all income was earned by households earning more than $200,000 a year. The median household income has been decreasing since it hit its peak in 1999, while top-earners' yearly incomes continue to grow. During this same period, the income of the middle class rose only 4 percent.

The middle class was responsible for the growth of interior design after World War II. Middle-class individuals may have budgeted or planned their projects a room at a time, but they did a lot for the profession. They helped build up the design business, forming a good base for volume.

While the middle class as a whole is a less significant part of our client base due to decreased income, there are those whose changed circumstances make them loyal customers. For example, the ones who have acquired income through an inheritance or other source and will sometimes want to use that money as part of a long-term investment. They will put a sizable part of their money into their homes as part of the building process because they view it as an opportunity for long-term financial growth. Other middle-class individuals will invest in areas they see as making a big difference in their lifestyle, such as their personal spaces, bathrooms, and master bedroom. Kitchens have now become a center for social interaction with family and friends, an extension of the family room and entertainment areas. They are no longer a hidden service area, but a major activity area in the home. The kitchen allows families to share culinary experiences. A lot of investment is being made in this area. Large investments are also being made in children's rooms, which previously were not considered important in a client's budget. People want to give their children experiences they themselves did not have. They're willing to invest in their environments.

THE WAY WE LIVE

My own experience in the design industry has changed dramatically throughout the years. Some of the changes were forced upon me, but looking back, I can say that it's probably been very good for my growth as a designer. These changes encouraged me to approach design in a very different way. They extended my knowledge base as well as my work opportunities.

Early in my career I had a lot of clients who came in every year to do a room or a project. This gave us a nice running base. Then the client list started to drop; however, our projects were larger and more expensive, involving custom merchandise and original proprietary design. This meant we weren't selling merchandise off the floor, so we had to change the structure of our studio. There was no point having a large investment in inventory that wasn't turning over.

As social and cultural trends changed through the years, so did the demands for interiors. At one point, country clubs, health clubs, and restaurants became an important part of people's daily experiences. Some people used their houses strictly for sleep and storage, which meant that they weren't investing extensively in their living spaces. Later, creating a home was much more important. They were used for entertaining. People wanted their house to be a safe haven, a retreat—a place for recreation, rejuvenation, and nurturing. Faith Popcorn's term "cocooning" applies.

People use rooms differently today. Bedrooms are often considered mini-retreats, sanctuaries, or special areas that reflect the individuality of each person in the house. According to Dr. Michael Solomon, human sciences professor of consumer behavior at Auburn University, when people buy a new home, they're not just moving. They're often buying different living situations and so need furnishings that address these different needs.[2]

Many more people are working at home, doing all types of work. Their home office is not always an extension of the office, but more often a primary production area. Years ago office furniture companies were producing what they called "home office furniture." Now we're realizing that some of the very finest "executive" and production furniture is being worked into these home spaces. It's fascinating to see the differences between the working environments people create for themselves. Their styles are most innovative and so often very individually productive. We can learn a tremendous amount from the different types of design we see developing in the arena of home offices.

WHAT DO CLIENTS WANT?

Clients want experiences. Often they want change, or they need it for a particular reason. Something may have happened in their lives that makes them say, I want a clean slate. Some clients also want to enjoy tradition. They love things that remind them of certain parts of their pasts.

Buying furniture is an emotional as well as a financial investment. Although designers are very concerned with function and safety issues, clients make most decisions based on emotions. Interior designers must continue to recognize and work with the emotional aspects of their field.

Many clients are willing to change, as long as the change is an improvement. People adapt astonishingly quickly to new things. We're all ready to invest as long as we see a reason to buy something new.

There are so many television shows today featuring "interior design." Clients' reactions to this can be interesting. In some cases they'll say, I don't want that [an object on a show]. I want something that's real and makes sense. They don't want something that's just for show. In other cases, clients are very influenced by some of the particular features they see on TV. We as designers are challenged to take the information they gather through TV or the Internet and adapt it to a real living and working environment. Sometimes this is a much more difficult task than one might expect. It's especially hard when a project is presented on television in such a way that it looks as though it was completed in one day by a few people, when it really took months and a large staff. Often the announcer explains that the cost was "minimal," which is really a matter of what one considers affordable.

It's also fascinating to see the values created through this kind of exposure. Some items shown on TV are opulent, while others are extremely inexpensive. This is causing a lot of confusion in today's market. It's one reason we all need consultants we can trust. Whether these consultants are in design, or any other allied field, we need to have someone we can compare notes with. Take, for example, medicine or law. We're exposed to so much information every day, which we find interesting, valuable, or maybe even necessary. But is this information really necessary or even correct? We need a professional person we trust to talk with and compare notes. Likewise, our clients need us.

There are more specialty shops opening today with exceptional products. They range from the chains, such as Williams-Sonoma and Bed Bath & Beyond, which have large quantities of products, to the exclusive specialty shops, such as those on Madison Avenue and other prestigious locations through the country. These are fine linen shops that have products of incredible quality and detail, and prices far beyond what we're accustomed to seeing. Clients are coming home with linens like these fully aware that they're luxury items—and that is what they want. They're seeing and tasting luxury things in so many different ways. As designers, we're challenged to work with these luxury items and to show our clients how to properly use and maintain them.

Clients are often confused by the mass market. They're looking for a resource that seems secure and reliable; they want a reasonably good selection and the assurance that what they see is the best in the industry. They also want a guarantee that the manufacturer or someone stands behind that furniture should anything go wrong.

In his book *The Paradox of Choice*, social scientist Barry Schwartz states that when clients have too many choices, they suffer. They come to designers because they want us to review the options in order to help them make appropriate decisions and eliminate chaos and confusion.

Customers today are concerned with value. They know quality is available and not just at the highest price level. Design clients know that technology has lowered the cost of many furnishings.

Snobby sales staff were often part of many status businesses, such as art galleries, exclusive clothing stores, and design studios. They were often rude and condescending to clients. Today, this is not accepted.

Consumers expect designers and salespeople to be able to answer questions. People don't want an uninformed body to point out that the furniture is attractive. They can see that for themselves. They want to know why the piece is great and why it should be part of their lives. They're asking for technical information, and most consumers are savvy enough and have the background to understand it.

This face-to-face interaction with retailers is no longer the primary setting for the shopper. Often clients go online and do a great deal of research before they come to us. They review magazines, watch television shows, and look at different hotels and resorts they've been to—here and around the world—before approaching designers. They often come with professionally prepared references and feel this is what they want. Sometimes these wants can be accommodated; in other cases the scale or direction may be something that requires considerable modification to fit the particular needs and situations of these clients.

Clients can be very impatient. Sometimes they want what they want, and they want it now. Their expectations are often that products serve their desired purpose exactly and that these objects also be fun to experience. They often don't have patience for furnishings that don't meet their standards of quality or aren't exactly what they want.

Today, people who want to buy furniture look for designers and stores that offer them service as well as value. Value comes at every price point. Buying new furniture is an event and should have all the ceremony events deserve. Clients expect a wonderful experience when they work with a designer, whether it be in a studio or a furniture store. They expect to be comfortable and find the experience pleasurable and enticing. They expect simple desires to be catered to, such as the opportunity to sit in comfortable chairs and be served refreshments.

Clients also enjoy the way technology can enhance a presentation; most everyone today is intrigued by both the technology and artistic talents that they themselves may not possess.

Furniture stores speak of "threshold resistance," a physical or psychological barrier that stands between the shopper and the inside of a store. Interior designers are very valuable to clients, so what's keeping clients from using us? What's the threshold resistance in interior design?

FORGING THE LINK

Today, people are looking for someone they can trust whose philosophy blends with theirs. Client's reasoning sounds something like this: Is this the kind of person I want to entrust my future to? I believe my future is directed by the environment I live in. I want to be sure the person who will be coaching me and helping me develop this environment is someone I can respect.

This attitude explains why clients must be considered part of the design team. In almost every professional relationship today, people don't want someone who tells them what to do, but a coach who considers them and makes suggestions.

Recent studies indicate that one pleasurable experience will offset the stress of three negative ones. If our mission is to improve the way people live, then turning the experience of working with an interior designer into a pleasure is a step in the right direction.

That means we have to work harder at preparing clients for the effects of change. Even though clients want what's new and different, change can come hard. People like things the way they used to be; it's comfortable. But change, no matter how difficult, is part of the process.

Design really isn't easy. Let your clients understand design is your mastery. You put a considerable amount of effort into it. Often we make things sound so simple that clients don't appreciate our efforts and, therefore, question the time and expense involved in the process.

Learning from the Starbucks Experience

In his recent book, *The Starbucks Experience*, Joseph A. Michelli, Ph. D., explains that the Starbucks Company believes in concentrating on the basics.[3] First of all, the company is interested in creating an experience. Starbucks offers all of its employees stock options and health insurance—even part-timers. The company spends more time on training than it does on advertising to make sure that its "partners," as Starbucks calls them, are familiar with the products and understand the meaning of good customer relations. Partners are also trained in empowerment strategies.

Starbucks has a turnover rate 120 percent below the average for the quick-service restaurant industry. Partners are encouraged to have fun and find out what the customers like and dislike, treating them as individuals and treating each other with respect. Partners are encouraged to make the company their own and feel part of it. Starbucks believes everything matters, from quality and every detail of the production process to the environment. The company aims to surprise and delight.

What a wonderful thing it would be if designers would emulate Starbucks—adding a bit of surprise and excitement to everything we do, turning the negative into positive opportunities, and leaving our creative and individual marks on every project. We want to be sure clients understand our commitment and the something special we add with each effort.

USER-FRIENDLY DESIGN STUDIOS

Studios and design centers must be more user-friendly and comfortable today. The entire experience must be fresh, educational, and fun. We have to use the communication techniques people have grown to expect. Design centers and studios must create reasons for customers to return so they'll continue to see these centers and studios as an ongoing resource.

Clients have been over-marketed. Everyone is trying to win a project. Companies that built their businesses by making cold calls no longer find cold calls effective: everyone is calling. Design marketers recommend that we develop clients, not projects, and create cradle-to-grave relationships.

Convenience is essential. Depending on the type of client, designers or stores may need to adjust their working hours to fit their customers' needs. We must find ways of coordinating our lives so we have time for our families and other interests. Many times we have to move away from "traditional" hours.

With fewer large furniture stores, many design studios have grown somewhat in size. Many have some inventory so clients can test pieces—especially upholstered furniture. Clients today are looking for style, but comfort is important to them as well, especially in certain pieces. Our studios need space for presenting these products, or a convenient location to take clients to try out these items.

There's greater power in association today. Independent designers and small companies tend to have ties to larger companies or are part of a network of other design studios or companies. Smaller firms often partner with manufacturers to present their products. The larger manufacturers can offer the warranties and guarantees that are of great importance to today's consumers.

This association benefits all those involved. Designers are in direct contact with the consumers and can pass information onto the manufacturers. Constant consumer feedback can be analyzed to give design directions. Manufacturers assist the retail or design firm with the in-depth customer service needed to keep clients happy for life.

> *We are sure to judge a woman in whose house we find ourselves for the first time, by her surroundings. We judge her temperament, her habits, her inclinations, by the interior of her home. We may talk of the weather, but we are looking at furniture.*

> — ELSIE DE WOLF,
> *THE HOUSE IN GOOD TASTE*,
> Century Books, 1913

AREAS OF INFLUENCE

When a designer and a client come together, both should understand that they bring their own experience, requirements, restrictions, and emotions to the project. Clients are influenced by many issues, not just their environments. Everything we're exposed to in life has influence, whether positive or negative. As designers, we need to get close enough to our clients to understand what experiences they've had in their lives, what these have meant to them, and how they will affect the project.

A number of my clients have been to design school, where they developed their visual skills. They also have been exposed to a great many parts of the interior design business. Their education may have been different from mine. Obviously, they didn't spend thirty-some years working in the field as I have or as some of you may have. Their work and life experiences are different, and this affects the way they view and think about design.

In fact, it's exciting to see these different ideas coming into play. A client with a design background brings different influences and experience to a project than one from another background. The experience of both is different from your own, and you must take this into account, even though you might have gone to the same school. Clients are experts on their particular areas of interest. Clients may know more about French antiquity of a certain period than the designer. However, the training and expertise of the designer will make him or her able to adapt period pieces or unique styles to the current-day working environment. In this instance, the client may be the consultant on a particular historic period, working with a professional interior designer.

It's hard not to be impressed, or at least influenced, by the projects published by the "shelter" magazines—*House & Garden, Architectural Digest, Southern Accents, Dwell,* and others. Clients come to us saying they want a room like the one in *Architectural Digest.* Often the size, scale, and total design of their space is very different from the one featured in the publication, not to mention the potential difference in budget. The cost of the home in the magazine may be twenty times the investment they have to make. While most people realize the owner of the home in *Architectural Digest* may be a bit wealthier than they are, they don't realize the huge investments made in properties. It can be difficult to explain to clients that there is a wide variation in budget.

We can explain these differences and offer to take influences and elements from that room to create a room that fits the way the client lives as well as his or her budget. Discussions of this sort can build a comfort level between designer and client, which allows for a better working relationship; the disparity between budget and reality doesn't have to be a major stumbling block.

Television and films are major influences as well. *The Journal of Interior Design* (formerly the *Journal of Interior Design Education and Research*) published an article on this subject.[4] The authors conclude that the influence is direct and immediate, that high-exposure viewers of TV and films prefer lifestyle designs and low-exposure viewers prefer traditional designs. Corry and Thompson imply that the media may also influence the design education of students and ask who's responsible for the content of visual images. "Because designers are influenced by visual images, both consciously and subliminally, it may be prudent to teach design students to be aware of the potential influence popular film media may have," they write.

We're influenced, and so are our clients. We may have watched the same program as they did with a completely different viewpoint, but we must still deal with their reaction to what they saw.

Television and film are pervasive, and the realities they present are as untrue as you can get with cameras. Sets for television shows are designed to tell a story and to entertain, not to create a space in which people live. And of course, no living room set for a televised series is ever cluttered.

Influences can be positive or negative. Some people might see a television show and be inspired to expand the space they have. Seeing something better than what you have will often make you want it. People may look at sets designed for television shows—which are kind of simple—and realize the clutter that they live with is perhaps eroding their thinking patterns. They realize they need a simpler environment. Or the set may just make them want to redesign.

Years ago, one of my projects was critiqued by a client's seven-or eight-year-old grandson, an avid television watcher. He visited her house when the project was almost complete, with the exception of a few final touches. He commented that this was a real Ewing room (from the show *Dallas*). She laughed, because she had never thought of the room in that light; in fact, the style was very different. The grandson thought the Ewing rooms were great, and he liked her room. It was his way of complimenting her.

Just as design has been influenced by such media as television, architecture in this country been influenced by that of other countries. The styles in Hershey, Pennsylvania, reflect several origins. Milton Hershey went to Cuba and returned to build his Moorish-style hotel. Many other buildings in Hershey show the influence of his visits to Cuba. As a Bostonian, his wife Catherine Sweeney Hershey had a significant influence on many of the buildings in that city as well.

We're also influenced by the people we live with. Early in my marriage, my husband said he loved a certain wallpaper pattern and wanted it in our master bedroom. It would not have been my selection, but the marriage was new. And because I had selected most of the furnishings in our house, I felt there should be something of his choice. I did the walls the way my husband wanted them. What a mistake! He had no idea how a small swatch of wallpaper translated onto a large mass of space. He didn't like the result, and I surely didn't. It was one of the first things I changed.

It's important for interior designers to guide our clients in their choices—to recognize what has influenced them and to counteract these influences when appropriate. One reason people hire designers is to make sure they don't put the wrong piece of fabric on a chair or the wrong wall covering in a certain space. Clients come to us because they want to use our experience and our eyes to select the right design elements and use them in the appropriate places.

But attitudes and opinions change over time. Anthony Torres is a designer newspaper editors loved to quote (and he has used his influence well). He said it's a good idea to let children have whatever color room they want. It's very inexpensive to paint a child's room. If the child decides to live in a red room, let him or her have that experience. When children grow up they'll have a much more mature attitude toward colors. Torres also said that if you really feel the color is awful, make it the accent color for the room—use it in a pillow, bedspread, or lamp so the child sees his or her opinions count. It's important to use as many of the child's choices as possible.

Everything influences us in one way or another. Some people are influenced a great deal by an article in the newspaper. Other people might read the article and forget it; it means nothing to them. I may save an article because one line in it makes me think by alerting me to a forgotten issue or one I was unaware of. The way I use that one line could be entirely different from what the article meant. This is how influence works.

We gain experience through travel, study, and observation. People tend to like the styles and furnishings of people whom they like, and have an aversion to the styles of people don't. All of this influences the interior spaces that we and our clients want to live with.

Notes

1. Lisa Johnson. *Mind Your X's and Y's: Satisfying the 10 Cravings of a New Generation of Consumers.* New York: Free Press, August 29, 2006.
2. Michael R. Solomon. *Consumer Behavior,* Seventh Edition. Englewood Cliffs, NJ: Prentice Hall, 2006.
3. Joseph A. Mitchelli, Ph.D. *The Starbucks Experience.* New York: McGraw Hill, 2006.
4. Shauna Corry and Joanri Asher Thompson. *The Journal of Interior Design,* Volume 19, No. 2, 1993, p. 31.

CHAPTER 7

DESIGN FIRMS

The interior design profession has existed for more than a hundred years. Designers have worked in many different ways, but one thing we have always had in common is an independent spirit.

PATTERNS OF SUCCESS

There are many business patterns that can lead to success in interior design. One method is to specialize in a particular area. Specialty design firms and their designers handle all the requirements of a particular client base, and there are different kinds of specialization. For example, those designing only retirement centers understand, in detail, all the medical, physical, psychological, and cultural needs of that demographic. Those designing for education often will specialize in elementary, secondary, or advanced education, so all their research and all the details and products they use are suitable for that area. A designer who does only lighting design would have lighting sources far more extensive than the average designer. As we review the extensive number of specialties later in this book, you'll notice that each one has its particular definitions and requirements.

A second pattern of success is hinged upon efficiency of production. These designers deliver their products with ease and speed. They have a defined business program, which enables them to produce a design with minimal effort.

Thirdly, very creative designers who do unusual design work are able to command considerable fees. They often do work that no one else knows how to do.

The final approach is defined by designers who partner with their clients. They become an intricate part of the client's business, professional office, or personal lifestyle. These designers are such important players in the lives of their clients that the clients can't imagine their lives without them.

Keys to Success in Business Today

To be a success, you must be intelligent and well educated. You need to be able to handle any problems that arise, analyze them, and find answers. You need to be able to prioritize issues in an order that makes sense to the people working with you.

- Communication skills are critical. Whether you're communicating verbally or on paper, you need to be able to look at a situation and explain it to people in a way that's reasonable. It's so important to be clear when speaking with other people.
- Motivational ability. You need to be able to get started and direct your own abilities in a way that creates a profitable approach to doing business; you need to get the right people, products, and structure in place to get the job done. Once a system is in place, we don't have to repeat processes. One person in the firm may begin a project and make sure the details are accurate, which forms a good basis for everyone else in the firm to continue to work. But you also need to direct people around you in a very positive and easy-to-follow way.
- Being organized. What the NCIDQ and other tests principally measure are organizational skills. It's so important for us to be organized and put things into an order, not just for ourselves but for our family and everyone around us.
- Humility. Many people have it when they're young; others never find it. Humility makes us more aware of other people's positions and therefore more sensitive to the different aspects of business and to the needs of any given moment. Above all, having humility means having respect for the people we work with, including our clients.

- Having proper support. It's wonderful to have your family's support, but often family members don't know your profession. A good business coach or consultant who works with you on a regular basis can keep things moving. That way you won't have great delays and disorganization blocking you from running your business smoothly.

THE INFORMATION GAP

A strong design practice is based on knowledge. You used to be able to count on adding to your knowledge incrementally, but the rate of change in the world today is phenomenal. Knowledge and education can prepare us to deal with these changes and can even equip us to be leaders in the field.

With the ever-growing pool of knowledge required for various specialties, practicing designers are increasingly realizing the need for additional training. They know there's tremendous value in specialized graduate programs. Educators may feel that designers don't appreciate the value of these programs. But based on my background with practitioners, I believe they do want additional education; they realize the need for it. Designers would like to continue their education, but it's not as easy for them to access it as it should be. Since most practicing designers must continue working, it's very difficult for them to take several years out of their practice to go back to a university campus and work on a specialty. They need programs that adapt to their work schedule and lifestyle.

We do have the benefit of conferences and specialized training, but it would be so valuable if this training complemented our basic education. The training should add knowledge to what we already have, rather than, as in some cases, duplicating or providing information unsuitable to the type of work we're doing.

The Joel Poisky/Fixtures Furniture Forum, Vision 2010 was an effort to bridge the gaps within interior design by bringing together educators, professionals, and the industry to review the knowledge they need to practice design today. The report resulting from the Furniture Forum stated, "The value of a well-designed environment is verifiable, making interior design a critical component of the designed environment ... the profession is supported by an expanding body of knowledge that encompasses business, art, and science."[1]

The members of our Designers' Business Forum have agreed unanimously that we want and need more education. As we grow in our individual specialties, we realize we particularly need education dedicated to the niches in our field.

Since that meeting of the Forum, numerous conferences, including several sponsored by ASID and IDEC, have looked at the different ways to update interior design education and bring it more in touch with our industry. I presented a proposal to IDEC suggesting that education needs to be coordinated between the practitioner, the industry, and the educational system. Each could support the other.

THE WAY WE WORK

In previous decades, one of the reasons large design firms were formed is transaction costs. The overhead for many standard business processes is so heavy that it's more effective to share the costs of office and communication procedures and bookkeeping. Today, almost any standard business procedures a design firm needs can be bought; there's no need to do it in-house. Services are available to handle payroll, accounting, bookkeeping, specification, billing, word processing, and finances. Design services, such as CAD and other highly skilled documentation and illustration work, are done virtually, often with specialists located in other parts of the world. Technology has made this communication possible.

As we've discussed, computers are no longer optional equipment for design studios; they serve every aspect of our businesses. Technology has eroded the requirements for the giant design firm. Working in very small teams or groups linked to a larger resource is often superior. Communications technology gives independent designers the means to link up with larger firms and still remain small, individual companies.

With technology, small firms are able to compete with large ones. They can often provide services that a single large firm can't. Due to their knowledge base and close business relationships, small firms are able to bring in expert knowledge from all over the world.

Social structures have changed the way we work. Designers are no longer the unquestioned authority. Today, most clients are knowledgeable about design, and they ask many, many questions.

Budgets are an issue for most of our practices today. There are many clients who can afford anything, but they usually want to know what it costs. Some clients will give a designer an open budget, but this isn't common in most markets. Many clients live very well and are willing to buy the best products available. There are others who are interested in quality designs, but the expense is a consideration.

Space is often an issue. It can be quite expensive in certain areas. Designers often move their practices to communities where they prefer to live and where they can afford the type of studio space and lifestyle they'd like to have. Since technology is permitting us to work almost anywhere, it's no longer necessary to be located in major cities or design areas.

In his book, *The Rise of the Creative Class*, Richard Florida speaks extensively about what attracts creative people to the places and things they really crave.[2] He points out that cities or towns have features attractive to creative people, who are no longer willing to live anywhere just because there's a job. Creative people want to have a lifestyle appropriate to their values. Often companies are forced to adapt, rather than demanding that creative people live and work in a particular location.

There's often a big difference between a person who has a creative idea and a truly creative person. If a person has one creative idea, and it doesn't work out, he or she is really in trouble. A truly creative person is working on many projects at one time so if one goes bad, there are still ninety-seven left to fall back on.

Florida goes on to say, "Creativity has become the most highly prized commodity in our economy." Creativity comes from people; it's not something a factory can produce. You can't say to someone, Come to work at 7:00 and be creative. You really need the right environment. Putting together the right people and the appropriate components fosters a creative climate as well as a good business environment.

Creativity is part of everything designers do. It's essential to our lifestyles and who we are. Different designers also need different support systems to maximize their creativity.

Florida also says "the enduring changes of our period are not technological, but social and cultural." We see that in so many ways. We also see that we as designers need experiences to stimulate us. Our clients are looking for experiences as well. They don't want the same old thing; they want something really new, creative, and exciting.

Creativity is often undervalued by designers themselves. Our clients see the value, but often we ourselves don't realize how important our creativity is to them. A number of years ago my firm did a marketing survey, asking our clients what they thought of the company. We expected them all to say it was well managed and efficient because we put so much emphasis on this. Not one client gave that answer. Maybe they took the business structure for granted. What they pointed out was the firm's high level of creativity and how it fit their style of living or working.

Even though small firms make sense in a lot of instances, large firms are experiencing a rebirth, especially those with a specialty. They're often able to take on and expedite projects quickly; they have the marketing and sales capability to generate the amount of business needed to support their quality design staffs. One of the difficulties of small studios is finding the time to design while simultaneously soliciting new business.

Gensler & Associates Architects is one firm that has spotted the changes and trends.[3] Gensler has put a lot of effort and used its management skills in redesigning the firm to fit today's needs. The firm has numerous offices throughout the country and has gained considerable business from the Pacific Rim. It continues to be a strong force in the field and valuable to our profession. So many other companies of similar stature are no longer in business or no longer the major competitors they were.

STYLE OF OUR FIRMS

The style of design firms has changed considerably. There are so many more cooperative companies than there once were. In the book *True North*, author Bill George states that leadership cannot be taught.[4] Leaders are shaped by personal experiences, often by crises in their backgrounds. They usually have a burning issue that's very important to them. Today's firms have a more collaborative management style, which is much more appropriate for the creativity of interior design. But George's position is still relevant. Although most successful firms today are much more collaborative, they still need the spirit of a leader. We need one person who really establishes the direction of the firm through a very different style than many of the dictatorial leaders of the past. It's also important as we look at our business structures that we integrate work with the other parts of people's lives. This gives them a chance to merge their professional and personal lives, including family, community, and friends. All of these become parts of a person's lifestyle. If designers don't have a good balance in their lives, their creativity suffers. This isn't good for the firm as a whole. It makes sense to create a schedule that permits us to have time and energy for the other parts of our lives.

MYSTIQUE VERSUS VALUE

Jerry Epperson, furniture-industry analyst and CEO of Harden Furniture in McConnellsville, New York, made a statement that we need to consider seriously. He's very angry with interior designers. Why? Because many designers aren't willing to help people understand how to use them. He said there's so much value in interior design, but the public, including his wife, doesn't know how to use—and is therefore uncomfortable using—interior designers. Epperson's wife will go out with her sister, select furniture, and bring it home. After a while, the two women will go shopping again and bring home something different. Epperson says he's not sure where all the previously purchased furniture goes. He wonders if his wife and sister-in-law used an interior designer, would they be more rewarded in their efforts?

Epperson knows that his home, as well as many other properties throughout the country, would be much more functional and attractive with the input of interior designers. Epperson feels we've been extremely negligent on our own behalf; we serve an important purpose, but the public doesn't understand our value.

If no one understands what we do, we must be doing something wrong. Very few people other than interior designers understand what we put into a project. That's partly because we're not explaining it well. It's also hard for even knowledgeable non-designers to understand what we do—not so much the creative part, but the process of making it all happen. Right now there are thousands of different definitions for an interior designer, depending on whom you ask. Even people who have worked with interior designers can't say what it is we do exactly.

Interior designers have two main functions. One is to educate our clients and retailers as to the type of products needed for a given installation. The second is to make it happen—to secure and complete the job in a skillful manner.

We must apprise our clients about what we do and how design affects their lives. We need to define interior design consistently, to educate people through our actions. More importantly, we need to explain the information in the language of the average consumer.

Paul Brayton, CEO of Brayton International, has often commented in lectures that it's time for designers and business people to work at seeing themselves as partners in a process that benefits everybody. According to Brayton, the competitive advantage of design is the intelligent application of resources to provide for human needs. And the market—the undifferentiated mass of potential clients—is very aware that one size does not fit all and demands customization of designs for local needs. Tom Peters, author of many books on business management, said during a presentation at High Point Market, "Design may be the most potent tool for differentiating one's products or services."

Peters is a strong advocate of explaining the value of design and how important it is to each and every business. Peters also says that design should take an equal and early seat at the head table, be on board at the creation of a dream, and an equal partner throughout. Peters is entirely correct. He learned this through the experience of working with a designer on his book.

Where interior design fails is in communicating its value. We have to start educating people about that value, and we can't do that unless we ourselves believe interior design is worthwhile. Long ago, the architectural profession redefined itself to exclude interior design; this doesn't make interior design any less valuable. Interior design may be a crazy amalgam of science and art, but its effects are measurable.

More than one designer has suggested that educators and practicing professionals collaborate on developing design lectures and public exhibitions in order to raise awareness that well-designed facilities can enhance the quality of life.

Cheryl Duvall, past IIDA president, also spoke at High Point and suggested that interior designers should comment on all kinds of environments—uncommon or not. When you're in a doctor's office that has a great waiting room, say so. When a store design makes you want to go in and shop, talk about it. If a space is attractive and accommodates the physically impaired, compliment the owner's grace and sensibility.

Certain issues are unavoidable for us as designers but their tie-in to interior design may not be obvious to the consumer. You can't go a week without seeing a television program or reading a newspaper story about repetitive stress injuries, indoor air quality, worker productivity, and the Americans with Disabilities Act. Talk with your friends and family about how your workplace addresses these issues.

Recently, Paul O'Neill, the former U.S. Treasury Secretary, was speaking about health care costs.[5] He claims that up to 50 percent of the health care spending in the United States provides no medical value. O'Neill argues that a large percentage of that money is lost in process-related problems, citing situations in which nurses are spending half of their time hunting for equipment or preparing equipment that should have been ready. O'Neill said the goal of our medical system should be to identify how to improve the processes and spread those practices to all providers. The process-related issues are design issues, not only medical or managerial ones. Interior designers would be very valuable in assisting hospitals in these processes. Think of how much we could improve our medical system if we took that "50 percent" and put it where it belongs.

Marilyn Farrow, past president of IIDA, said in a presentation to designers at NeoCon, a commercial interior furnishings conference and exhibition, that designers should measure the differences in their clients' productivity after the work environment has been newly designed. They should provide statistics from the perspective of the client, not the designer. When we give corporate clients examples of success stories, they should be expressed in the boardroom.

"What isn't being offered to the client is the type of information developed through case studies," Farrow asserted during her presentation. "The client isn't aware of how we improved productivity, reduced absenteeism, and lowered employee turnover by creating a safe, productive, healthy, and accessible environment, unless designers tell them."

Design awareness has to be taught, and it should be taught in kindergarten and elementary schools as part of the basic curriculum. In social studies, teachers can discuss how Frank Lloyd Wright tried to change the way secretaries sat by designing three-legged chairs for the secretarial pool at Johnson Wax. In history, they can talk about why the senate chambers have very high ceilings and how this affects the way Senators behave toward each other. When the effects of light are discussed in science class, teachers can mention that choosing specific lighting for various functions is part of the work of interior designers.

On the level of higher education, Harvard Business School teaches case histories involving industrial design. Why not teach interior design case histories as well?

We also need to define interior design in terms of market expectations. We have the information. All we have to do is pull it together and make it accessible.

INTERIOR DESIGN IS AN ART AND A SCIENCE

God is in the details.

—LUDWIG MIES VAN DER ROHE

Interior design may have started as the child of decorative arts and architecture, but that was over a hundred years ago. Many sciences have contributed to the body of knowledge of design.

Are we designers or artists? Roger Yee, past editor of *Contract Design* magazine, asks in an editorial, "Are designers trained to see themselves as artists conversant with technology, whereas society wants them to perform more like technicians who are facile with art?"[6] It's not that simple, Mr. Yee.

Interior design is a service industry, and practicing interior designers are trained observers—just like doctors, sociologists, and other social scientists. Behavioral psychologists make recommendations based on their observations; so do interior designers.

Knowledge and education are crucial elements of being a designer. In the past one hundred years, the field has both narrowed and broadened. Designers need more in-depth technical knowledge today. It's no longer possible to be a generalist. At the same time, our understanding of the work is deeper and wider. Interior design was never just about selecting pretty fabrics. It was always about using spaces to support a range of human activities.

Interior design is rooted in the practical. Elsie de Wolfe may have been "the Chintz Lady," but suitability, simplicity, and proportion were as important to her as beauty, comfort, and peace of mind. People tend to forget that. It's true that author Edith Wharton (with architect Ogden Codman) wrote the first book on interior design, *The Decoration of Houses*, to alleviate the boredom and frustration of her marriage. It's true that de Wolfe was almost forty when she first sought design clients. It's also true that after World War I, it became fashionable in England for women to have careers as interior designers, and that interior design was a way for the middle class to buy into an aristocratic way of life.

To characterize interior design as the profession of bored housewives catering to the nouveaux-riches and wannabes is a lie by omission. Practicality has been as much a part of interior design through the years as beauty. Interior design has become "democratized." We have always worked with people, but the spectrum of our clients has broadened over the years.

Interior designers have been described as operating at a pre-empirical intuitive level, but we don't really design only by hunch and guesswork.[7] Much of our so-called intuitive knowledge has been documented through a discipline known as "human factors," the study of how people relate to their interior spaces (also sometimes known as "proxemics"). Human factors also draw on acoustics, illumination, olfaction, kinesthetics, ergonomics, color psychology, cultural bias, anthropology, and sociology.

The designer is not a mystic, dictator, or god. An interior designer should operate in the same manner as a physician who's a team member in helping solve your medical problem. You don't walk into a doctor's office and accept everything he or she says as absolute, as patients did in the past. But you do respect the doctor's experience. The doctor bears the responsibility for bringing you the right treatment. As designers, we're responsible for bringing the right type of design to the public.

But what constitutes the "right type of design" is subject to change. What we believe are the standards of the day can be completely different tomorrow. A scientific discovery or current events, proprietary research from manufacturers, an industry white paper, or newspaper reports of business trends can change the standards of our work.

A great deal of information is available to us; we are responsible for incorporating it into all our design projects. Our work shapes our environments. We are, in effect, leaders of human behavior. Sometimes this information is hard to obtain. As a consequence, some designers unknowingly create environments that encourage wrong behaviors. It's our responsibility to create the best environments we possibly can.

FINANCE

Many interior design, architectural, and engineering firms have been seriously undercapitalized. That means it's been easy to enter the business, but often very difficult to succeed. Running a business from home, starting small, and planning carefully to position yourself financially and professionally is common in the industry. A design business also allows people to nurture their skills and talents and cultivate the business into a job that pays well.

More than 50 percent of interior design businesses are owned by women. That's a good thing because businesses started by women may have had the edge in times when little credit was available, according to a February 21, 1992 article in the *Wall Street Journal*. Three out of four women entrepreneurs started with their own financing. They couldn't get credit in the 1980s. But in the 1990s, when banks began calling in loans, these women weren't adversely affected because they had no loans to call in.

In that same article, a past director of the Small Business Administration offers another reason businesses run by women may have an edge even during a recession. "Women are not the risk-takers that men are," says Alice Brown. "They are more likely to start smaller than men, with less debt, less overhead, less everything."

Today, interior design firms need more to start up and keep running. We need equipment and capital, which is often not easy to secure without prime financing. Although clients do give us retainers, it's not proper to pay our day-to-day operating expenses with our clients' money.

It's well known that in the past, many interior design firms were poorly run financially, which is one of the reasons it's so difficult for interior design firms to get credit even today. There is a much greater need for careful management of each account; there's also a greater respect for good financial management in general. If you don't have the money to run a business properly, you must consider other ways of working.

Even well run, efficient firms need changes in their current systems. Is there a way we can join another firm to be more efficient? Can we reduce overhead by moving to shared spaces? We have to constantly look for ways of doing better work at less cost.

Credit and Payment

One of the sore points in this industry is that credit is available to everyone else. But when designers ask for credit with manufacturers, there's very little of it available. Today, most clients are expected to pay a retainer or a deposit—often pro forma, which means they pay for the merchandise before it's delivered. This practice is standard in many large cities, but the clients of designers in smaller communities aren't used to it. Clients want to see the merchandise. Most clients don't want to pay for expensive custom merchandise until they examine it and see that it's in good condition. Credit card payments are common because they give clients some recourse if an item doesn't meet their expectations.

When establishing the standards of their firms, designers must decide how they want to handle their credit systems. They have to decide whether they want to be responsible for accounts receivable or to use an expediting company or other systems for clients to purchase furniture, while the designers simply accept fees for their services. The choice strongly depends on the type of clients they're dealing with, the structure of their companies, and the risks involved.

Some firm services include the design and procurement of products used, especially in medium-size jobs. That means these firms are also responsible for securing credit for their jobs. It is their credit or financial structure that will determine the credit terms or payment system set for the projects by the various suppliers, not the finances of the clients. This gives the client a completed project and a standard payment process.

The decision about handling credit may not be one the designer can make. Some suppliers prefer to sell directly to the client and expect the designer to be paid a fee by the client. Some suppliers provide servicing guarantees in the client's name.

A good financial structure is critical for any professional office. We must be sure the way we design the finances of our firm complements the professional services we're offering.

Compensation

Compensation of staff or associates comes in many forms today, but it is far more performance-based than ever before. Staff people expect to participate in the profits of the company. They're often reluctant to participate in its losses. It's important for firms to structure their business so that staff people see themselves as an integral part of the company. Employees are able to produce work that generates better profits if they understand the structure.

In many cases, interior designers won't be on salary to a single firm but will consult and work with many firms throughout the country. This is the trend in other industries, and it is also part of ours.

This means that we must develop compensation plans, especially in the areas of entitlements (insurances, retirement plans). Ideally, medical insurance and retirement benefits will not be tied to the company but to the individual. Professional associations can be very helpful in offering health, insurance, and retirement plans to give individuals the benefits that previously were available through only large corporations.

Accounting

Design firms are handling a larger volume of business—both large and small accounts—much more quickly.

The cost of managing projects may change whom we accept and keep as clients. One reason design firms continue to lose money is that they do too much for what they are being paid. Not every project requires the same intensity of effort and involvement. Design firms need work at a variety of levels. We need to determine what level of work the client wants and expects, then charge according to our responsibilities on the project.

Staying in business isn't about just getting accounts; it involves looking at which accounts are price-effective. One design firm found that some accounts were too expensive to handle. It suggested to those clients that they either enlarge the account or use another firm. As a result, the firm lost $120,000 worth of business, but it had cost the firm $150,000 a year to manage those accounts. By eliminating these accounts, the firm gained a net profit of $30,000.

Mary Ann Bryan, FASID and an interior designer, believes that the mindset of designers makes them uncomfortable to speak directly about money, even when they're successful and efficient in handling clients' money and budgets. As she has stated in conference speeches and numerous articles, Bryan attributes the problematic mindset to a sneaking belief that what designers do isn't worth paying for.

Money is a measure of success. The effects of design are an abstraction. The problem lies in translating these abstracts into a dollar value. Clients today associate everything with cost. They also believe if something is great, it must be expensive. Many design firms haven't learned how to convert that belief into an appropriate presentation that makes clients want to encourage our best work or to be willing to pay for it.

Because the market and the services we offer are changing, the charging system of a design firm needs to be reviewed on an annual basis. The review should consider the type of jobs done, the staff involved, and the execution process. It's amazing how a slightly different interpretation can make the difference between an understanding and accepting attitude, versus a doubtful and difficult one. Our systems must adapt to the market today.

Profit Ratio

There are many different ways of running profitable firms. One needs to consider the definition of profit. Is it just money, or is it having the right clients, doing great work, and having the lifestyle to go along with it? As you consider your design firm, you need to look at the requirements of your lifestyle. Is your business supporting your family and others? What are the demands? What work are you doing to generate this income? What is the market today, and where do you stand with regard to your staff and products? Often design firms are in the position to add services their clients need, which also increases their profit. Ideally, this can be done with minimal additional effort and still supply clients with products they very much need and want.

Notes

1. "Vision 2010," *Interiors and Sources*, June 1994, p. 20.
2. Richard Florida. *The Rise of the Creative Class*. New York: Basic Books, 2002.
3. Glenn Rifkin. "Efficiency, Not Ego, Gives Edge to Design Firm," *New York Times*, April 10, 1994, p. F7.
4. Bill George. *True North*. San Francisco: Jossey-Bass, 2007.
5. Reed Abelson. "In Bid for Better Hospital Care, Heart Surgery With a Warranty," *New York Times, May 17, 2007*.
6. Roger Yee. "Are You an Artist or a Designer?" *Contract Design*, June 1993, p. 8.
7. Robert Sommer. *Personal Space: the Behavioral Basis of Design*. Englewood Cliffs, NJ: Prentice-Hall Spectrum, 1969.

CHAPTER 8

A MISSION FOR THE INTERIOR DESIGN FIELD

*"I have always found," said Mr. Pullman,
"that people are greatly influenced by
their physical surroundings. Take the
roughest man, a man whose lines have
brought him into the coarsest and poorest
surroundings, and bring him into a
room elegantly carpeted and finished,
and the effect on his bearing is immediate.
The more artistic and refined the external
surroundings, the better and more
refined the man."*

—RUSSELL LYNES,
THE TASTEMAKERS

At the recent LightFair held at New York City's Javits Center, almost an entire floor was filled with just light bulbs. I've never seen so many different kinds of bulbs. We're looking at energy conservation opportunities that are beyond anything we could have ever imagined—3,125 bulbs powered by one outlet. This is a perfect opportunity for designers to look for new innovations—not just little fixes, but big things—to create a new environment for all of us. The following are just a few examples. You can add others that fit into your practice.

INNOVATION

Innovation has come even to the simplest items. In 2006, there were toasters in many styles designed by Michael Graves, such as the Back-to-Basics Egg & Muffin Toaster, which sells for more than twice the price of an ordinary toaster. Such innovations made the toaster one of the top selling items in 2006. For those who are into multitasking, the Egg & Muffin Toaster is a perfect addition to the kitchen. We may have felt that a toaster was mundane. But any everyday object, including the toaster, can be made more interesting with the creative artistry and possibilities of such inventions.

Classrooms in Condominiums

Developers are bringing schools into condominium communities. They know if they want to sell condos, they have to meet the needs of residents. Too many people move out of condos to other residential areas during the years their children attend school. By bringing quality schools into condos, the developers are making these residential units much more desirable.

The Other 90 Percent

Recently there was an exhibit called "Designing for the Other 90 Percent" at Cooper-Hewitt Museum in New York City. The exhibit featured the many objects that can be manufactured inexpensively to fill the needs of the 90 percent of humanity usually neglected by top designers. Included is a "Life Straw"— a personal water purification device. The "Global Village Shelter" is designed for disaster relief; it offers interior comfort, privacy, and protection from the weather when traditional housing isn't available.

In his presentations, Paul Polak, president of the International Development Enterprise, has stated that 95 percent of the world's designers focus on developing products and services exclusively dedicated to the wealthiest 10 percent of our population. A revolution in design is needed to reach the other 90 percent.

TAKING RESPONSIBILITY FOR HEALTHY ENVIRONMENTS

A recent ASID publication stated that interior designers are responsible for specifying more than 90 percent of the materials and products used in buildings. That means we have the ability to create healthy environments and must be fully aware of the contaminant issues relating to these products. The presence of so many potential health hazards concerns us, especially because they are from common biological contaminants such as mold, bacteria, spores, viruses, dust, and combustible materials.

There are also products manufactured in an environmentally unfriendly way, creating gases and other pollutants. These products include tobacco, furnaces, fireplaces, automobiles, cooking appliances, and other equipment. Radon, still considered a major contaminant, can be contained if kept inside a building constructed over a radon source in the soil. VOCs—volatile organic compounds—are found in building materials, cleaning products, coatings, and other construction items, such as insulation, carpet, wallcovering and other textiles. Formaldehyde is often part of adhesive but can also be an ingredient in carpeting and insulation. Pesticides are also an issue.

Basically, we need to become aware of all the contaminants in the various materials we use. Because we are responsible for specifying these materials, we're in a position to seriously affect the health of our clients. Leadership in Energy and Environmental Design (LEED) gives us a rating system for many of these products. But beyond that, we need to research comprehensively the components of every product we use and be sure we understand their underlying health issues. We're often aware of what a fabric is made of but not the finishes applied to it. Unfortunately, a lot of this information is not as available as it should be. We have the responsibility to find it.

Flammability

Furniture, especially bedding, is strongly regulated for flammability standards. Our industry has been aware of these standards for a long time, but in the future there's going to be an even stronger emphasis. We can expect to see our clients request flammability standards on almost everything we use. We need to be very conscious of these standards because this is an area of designer responsibility that very much affects the projects we work on. We need to know the specifications of each product we use and the many different flammability codes.

Green Light Bulb Movement

The U.S. Department of Energy states that if every American home used a compact florescent lamp (CFL), it would save approximately 15 million tons of coal a year. Half of residential electricity comes from coal-fired utilities. General Electric has been promoting CFLs; we see them in every store. Fortunately, the price of these bulbs has been reduced; they now cost approximately $1.50 to $3 each instead of $15 to $20. The CFL bulbs also come in soft white, which is a lot more attractive than the color previously offered. This green light bulb movement could dramatically change lighting fixtures in most of the projects we do. Unfortunately, the trend is not yet at the forefront.

Sustainability

Manufacturers are starting to use sustainability as a major marketing tool. Companies speak about their membership in the Forest Stewardship Council (FSC), a certified Smartwood Program for the Rainforest Alliance, or the Sustainable Forestry Initiative. SFI membership means the timber is harvested and managed according to certain guidelines. SFI cuts and manages trees in a very responsible fashion.

It's also interesting to know that in 1900, according to SFI, 41 percent of the New York state was forest; today it's 52 percent. These environmental organizations are really encouraging the sustainability of our natural resources. Furniture companies are looking at sustainability issues as they relate to production. They are also examining the way raw materials are supplied in factory designs, finishing materials, and all the individual components that go into a piece of furniture to make sure they're not only sustainable but healthy for the end user.

Organic Leather and Fabrics

Organic issues have moved from the food industries into our textiles and other furniture products. We now have organic leather. A company in California sells organic leather made from the hides of wild animals or those raised to produce organic meat. This leather is often used in furniture and headboards. "Green" leather from free-range cattle is treated with vegetable dyes rather than processed with heavy metals.

There's even an Organic Trade Association, which has established standards for the processing of textiles. These standards exclude all heavy metals and components such as formaldehyde, but they do allow the use of synthetic sewing threads. There's also the previously mentioned Forest Stewardship Council, a non-profit organization that sets standards for environmentally responsible forestry practices.

Noise Pollution

Noise can diminish your concentration and productivity, and can even have an effect on your health. Good interior acoustical design can decrease most noise problems. I was asked to review a physician's office regarding the Health Insurance Portability and Accountability Act (HIPAA) issues a number of years ago. While I was in the physician's waiting room, I discovered there were not only privacy issues, which had concerned the physician originally, but also issues regarding staff spaces and noise levels. As I tried to read, my concentration kept being broken by everyday noise. Everything that went on at the receptionist's desk was too loud: the stapler, the shuffling of paper, the ringing telephone, the clatter of the typewriter. The speaker for the piped-in music was at her end of the room, and she had to speak over it when she used the phone.

At 11:45 a.m. when I heard the receptionist say she was getting a headache, I wasn't surprised; so was I. The acoustical design of the room amplified all normal sounds. With the exception of the carpet, every surface in the room was hard. The ceiling was very low above her desk, causing the sound to reverberate even more. Even the lighting was annoying. Two bright downlights bounced light off her desk.

Noise is simply unwanted sound. Although we aren't comfortable in complete silence, the level and type of noise we are subjected to should be controlled for optimum productivity. Fortunately, today, we have professionals skilled in many systems. Acoustical design needs to be part of every space we work on.

When I was doing a program for the Austin Corporation in Cleveland, I experienced the ultimate in acoustical design for lecture halls. Before the program began, I was on stage and speaking quietly about personal things to a friend I had not seen for several months. Later I learned that everyone in the hall, even those in the back row, could hear every word we had said. It is the sign of a very well designed lecture hall when the speaker can talk at a normal volume without a microphone and be heard clearly by everyone.

Good interior design is responsible design. It takes into account the needs and realities of the situation and of the people who will use the space. This approach to interior design looks to the future rather than waiting for a problem to occur. It goes beyond beautification or responding to environmental issues raised by the media. When we address real needs with well-researched solutions, interior design is indispensable.

DESIGN AFFECTS BEHAVIOR

Environments direct human behavior. Interior designers have a responsibility to design spaces dedicated to the needs of people of varying ages and physical abilities and for all types of activities—private, work-related, and communal.

The concept that interior design can change the way people live and think is older than the field of itself. The Willow Tearooms, designed by Charles Rennie Mackintosh, were apart of a project to fight drunkenness in Glasgow at the turn of the century. In his book, *Interior Design and Decoration*, Sherrill Whiton said a goal of interior design was "to produce a unified composition and a desired aesthetic and psychological effect."[1]

"Virtually everything that man is and does is associated with the experience of space," wrote anthropologist Edward T. Hall in 1966.[2] In 1969, psychologist Robert Sommer wrote, "designers are shaping people as well as buildings."[3]

Interior design educator John Pile wrote in 1988, "Human beings are powerfully affected by their particular environment, and . . . human behavior is in turn affected by the environment in which it occurs."[4]

The effect of environment on behavior is proved by every project we do. In over twenty-five years of working with the Milton Hershey School in Hershey, Pennsylvania, I have seen interior design help change lives. Children from deprived, neglected, and destructive backgrounds who came to the school left the nurturing environment later as accomplished professionals with personal skills. In the pleasant and attractive Milton Hershey School environment, they are given a new way to live. From their clothing to the many activities they have the privilege of experiencing, everything works together to reinforce the new lives of these children.

A great many of these youngsters changed just because of the exposure to a controlled environment with furnishings geared toward their development. We made sure that everything from the chairs they sat on to the views they saw would enrich their educational and social development. The direction of this experiment in behavior was determined by noted psychotherapists, sociologists, educators, and the input of the students, aged five and up. The changes have been dramatic.

Founder's Hall at Milton Hershey is a particularly good example of an environment that changes behavior. People might be boisterous and loud outside, but once they come through the doors, they're perfectly silent. There are no signs requesting quiet; it's their reaction to the space. It's an awe-inspiring, dramatic building, which sets a tone of respect for the space, the institution, and the overall objectives of that institution. Part of the effect is due to the high ceilings and the sheer size of the interior space, the materials used, and the overall ambiance. Architects and designers employ this technique in other community buildings designed as areas of respect, celebration, and cultural enrichment.

Much church design has changed to accommodate a more participatory style of worship in which the congregation and ministers interact. (The Catholic Church is an extreme example of this.) Therefore, some church design, which worked well for an older philosophy and liturgical style, does not work for the new liturgy. We have moved from a mystical, hierarchical style of worship to a more egalitarian one, and church spaces are much more intimate than they were.

Environment Makes a Difference

Doesn't cultural deprivation lead to spiritual destruction? Today acute problems in human behavior include crime on the streets, teenage drug use and violence, and more. When you think of the homes these teenagers are coming from and the schools in which they're being educated, you see that not much is being done to develop their self-esteem. Because we know environment can make a difference, it seems that upgrading the environment would be an effective and inexpensive method of changing their world.

Some of these issues should be dealt with in design schools as a standard part of our training. Perhaps our professional associations should target this issue and challenge us to find solutions.

A local housing project wanted me to design and furnish one of its standard homes with a budget of $2,000. I thought it was a great opportunity for students and was able to involve a class of design students at the Ai Bradley Academy. Together, we established a budget for each room, evaluated likely storage needs, and set a schedule. After coming up with viable floor plans, the students shopped at the local Goodwill and other low-cost stores. They did the painting and installations themselves. At the completion of the project, the home looked terrific and worked well. The students gained practical experience. They loved doing the project; they didn't want to leave. They had done a great job. The residents of the project copied what the students did in their own homes. This design effort caused city standards to be raised for all the project homes in the city. It was an outstanding cooperative effort and all the result of design students, their professors, and our office.

According to Professor Leslie Kane Weisman, an associate professor of architecture at the New Jersey Institute of Technology and author of *Discrimination by Design: A Feminist Critique of the Man-Made Environment*,[5] a socially responsible design education is integral to the health and prosperity of design and architectural professionals and their clients.

Students in Weisman's course, "Architecture and Social Change," are required to volunteer twenty hours of community service to a nonprofit agency that addresses social problems dealt with in the course.

"When students realize they are responsible and account-able to others as designers, they begin to design in an empathic mode, allowing them to empower others through their work rather than merely imposing their own images upon the world," Professor Weisman says.

Professor Weisman spent ten years putting together her book, which discusses man-made space and how many spaces limit human beings and exclude, dismiss, and devalue women, minorities, and other marginalized groups. The book targets a whole realm of spaces in which designers and architects can rewrite public opinion of the design industry.

Use Design to Build a Sense of Community

*In its most basic form, a community
is a group of people who have made
a commitment to communicate with
each other at an increasingly meaningful level. At a more sophisticated level,
a community is a group that can speak
together with a unified voice.*

—DR. M. SCOTT PECK,
THE DIFFERENT DRUM

Some current design work is remarkable. Physical fitness centers allow moderate and extreme sports to be brought indoors so they can be pursued without the limitations of weather. What other activities could also be expanded through the use of interior space? We might build communi-ties around many types of shared activities and residents with common social and other denominators, instead of just golf courses or shopping centers.

The cities and towns of an earlier era compelled interac-tion. If you walked past a shoemaker's shop, you said hello. You could observe the behavior of people on many socioeconomic levels. It was possible for a needy child to emulate a doctor or a lawyer—the way they walked, talked, and interacted with people. You came into frequent contact with role models.

Today we are living in our own ghettoes with our own barriers. It doesn't matter whether you're a factory worker, a middle class professional, or a millionaire. Our developments and communities build boundaries that limit the contact we have with other people. Most of the people we meet and associate with are similar to us. This creates many limitations and, in a sense, builds walls among different types of people. When we build walls, history tells us that we create problems—even wars. If we're living together, we need areas that build community. One of the advantages of living in a large city such as New York is that you're forced to intermix with all types of people on a daily basis. It's amazing to see the extensive mix we come into contact with in the city every day. In the building I live in, twenty-eight different languages are spoken. I have had the privilege of being exposed to some social mores I probably would have never touched in any other way. It's been a beautiful growing experience.

Starting in the 1990s, major bookstores positioned themselves as hangouts or clubs. In one bookstore, I saw a nanny with two preschool children napping in a stroller as she sat and read. A retired gentleman sat at a table drinking coffee and comparing several books from a large pile. A group of college students discussed something in great detail and intensity at another table. This bookstore is now one of the best meeting spots. Somehow I had not thought of bookstores as a place for dating, but it has become an apparently popular one. Many of these bookstores have cafés, and people take large groups of magazines and books, sit there for hours reading, and meet their friends. A bookstore is definitely a social area for almost any community, be it a large city or small town.

Our work affects behavior whether we like it or not. Let's discuss how to create spaces that direct behavior appropriately.

Consider Special Needs

What should interior design be doing that it's not doing today? The field should be improving social dynamics for all people, not just the wealthy and the middle class. The sensory aspects of a space—how well we hear, how our vision is directed, and how we use all of our senses—need to be dealt with when designing spaces.

Walt Disney was a pioneer in creating physical demonstrations of this principle. In Disney World and at Epcot Center, it's not only what we see but what we touch, hear, and even smell. The experience is beyond the visual—it is all-encompassing. As a result, our receivers operate at a higher capacity. We see Walt Disney as the leader in experiential environments, but now it is the demand of almost everything we do.

What I care about is whether a particular environment meets the needs of the particular people who are using it. Five-year-olds should be put in spaces that are really suitable for five-year-olds, for example. Through designing educational facilities, I learned that different age groups respond differently to various environments. For example, younger children need much more stimulation through color to keep them excited and to give a fun feeling to a space, while older students may need a quieter space for longer periods of study. Can we provide the right environment for students studying calculus—one that enhances their ability to acquire knowledge? Are we giving ill people an environment that supports them—one that provides the most comfort possible? Does the environment give them a feeling of some control over the lighting and acoustics? We have to look first at human needs, not what we can do with buildings.

This is not to say I don't appreciate artistic buildings. We need monuments in our society. But a building dedicated to a specific function should work. The Frank Lloyd Wright Group designed a facility in Ohio for Alzheimer's patients. Typically, Alzheimer's patients have memory retention problems, and fear and rage are common results. The Group researched the kinds and sizes of spaces Alzheimer's patients are comfortable with. Rather than using colors and numbers to help identify rooms, the Wright Group placed a showcase at the entrance of each room housing the patient's own memorabilia. This made it easier for patients to identify their rooms and decreased the likelihood of confusion and paralyzing fear.

This is the way interior designers need to look at every person and every activity. We need to put the same amount of attention into studying the way people perform everyday activities, such as the way a mother holds her baby and the way people move on the street. These activities need the same kind of attention that has been devoted to studying pilots in the cockpits of airplanes to determine what holds their attention and what is ergonomically comfortable. There are a lot more mothers and babies than there are pilots.

Climate issues such as extremely heavy snow and ice storms make us realize we need to take action to develop changes in our streets and sidewalks so people don't fall and break arms and legs. We seem to be having some extreme weather issues, and this needs to be considered as part of our design elements. The heavy flooding in New Orleans has led to a lot of new design ideas. Hurricane Katrina has led to the enforcement of regulations, which include new window protections and buildings being raised above flood elevations. The wind load criteria have prompted the transformation of our building codes, forcing them to be much stronger and more durable in the face of extreme wind. Katrina has encouraged changes in many other parts of the country.

Escalating construction costs are followed by much higher insurance premiums. Probably one of the most important results of Katrina is the dramatic increase in energy costs, which have motivated clients to go with green buildings as a major part of their programs. Katrina has increased our national consciousness about energy costs.

The ramps added to many buildings for wheelchair access have often become obstacles for people not in wheelchairs. Fortunately, some of the designs have improved, but there are many locations where the ramps are still a major issue. Designers must create a solution that works well for all users of the space.

Cynthia Leibrock, founder of Easy Access Barrier Free Design, agrees. She said in a speech: "Designers' knowledge of aesthetics allows them to integrate technology into the environment. No one with a physical difference wants to be stigmatized by that difference." It is exciting to see how designers have improved design, making it more universal and not simply an adherence to the ADA. It is design that is complementary to all of us, regardless of our size, age, or physical limitation. Many of these universal features have become much more attractive and user friendly.

Mall designs are being greatly improved, since in the past there were so many hazards with steps, ramps, and areas that made it so easy to fall or trip while looking at the store windows. Mall owners have also realized that they must be more experiential. They incorporate play areas for children, seating areas, and social gathering areas for waiting. Mall owners realize that if they are to be profitable in the future, the malls must be fun places to be as well as to shop and spend money.

The Human Factor in Private Spaces

Considering human factors in design means fitting clients with the right products. For instance, I took a married couple into a bathroom fixtures showroom and had them try different toilets. They tested the contours of the American seat versus the French to determine which contours were most comfortable. They tested different heights because, as people grow older, the height of a toilet becomes a critical issue. For the gentleman of the house, who is tall, we chose an eighteen-inch toilet. For the woman, who was not as tall, we chose one that was sixteen-inches.

The standard toilet in many dwellings is fourteen inches. This is not great for people as they age. It might be okay today, but give some individuals another ten years or so, and they're likely to find it a problem. People used to stay in a home seven to ten years. These particular clients have been in their present home for twenty-five years and are remodeling it because they like the neighborhood. I'm sure they will be there another twenty-five years. The time to deal with potential problems is now, when they are redesigning their home.

The plumbing business has realized that people want bathrooms that fit them, and has really taken advantage of this. Clients are spending amazing amounts of money and effort to design or upgrade their personal bathrooms, as well as the guest bathrooms.

Considering human factors is just good business practice. The point is that when a client wants a bathroom with unusual faucets, it's fine: the client is the only one who uses them. That client will soon learn how to turn the faucets on and off. But for public spaces or family spaces used by the visiting mother-in-law or grandfather, the faucets may not work. It may take the visitors awhile to figure out which is hot and which is cold. They could scald themselves if they turn the incorrect faucet.

We need to look at where artistry is appropriate. If it's in your own personal space, and you want something very different because it makes you smile every time you use it, that's wonderful! You'll learn its quirks; it won't be a problem. Attractive design doesn't always mean that it's functional and easy to use. When more than one person will use the space, I think we have to be more universal in our designs.

Design an Office that Works for Workers

Offices have changed considerably in many cases. We don't always just go to the office with a dedicated desk, cubicle, or private corner office anymore. Often, we go to a work environment where we work with other people and share experiences. We have certain tools that support us and that we're involved with. More than that, work is a social experience. The variety of designs and styles of offices today is exciting. We have seen a lot of experimentation in the last twenty-five years, taking offices from the standard, classic design to something beyond our imaginations. But many of these new offices work.

It's marvelous when people really consider what they're doing and find the most effective way of accomplishing their goals. The tools around them need to be altered in order to support their work. As designers, we work very closely with end users, facilities people, and professionals, as well as consultants. A team effort helps bring together many components that support our work.

It's been amazing to visit projects after completion and have the staff say, "I don't understand it—I'm no longer tired. I can go home and have plenty of energy to spend time with my children. My whole life has changed because my work environment is more effective. I am getting more done in less time, and I am not as fatigued." This is the kind of result we want each workspace to have, whatever the given task may be.

Office environments have physical, cultural, and psychological effects on human beings. We spend many hours every day working in our offices. Every component of the office environment spurs a human response. Those who design offices—whether they're professional architects, interior designers or facilities managers—must have input from other disciplines.

100

An executive whose firm had just moved into a new building told me an eerie story. Not a week went by without the wail of an ambulance. The company nurse said she had never seen so many instances of hypertension, depression, and absenteeism. There had been more visits to the health suite than ever before in the history of the company. Everyone had been excited to be in this beautiful, spacious, quality environment. Why was this happening?

In the brand-new building, everything was the same intensity, and gray without variation is boring and tedious. Color specialists say people become nervous and edgy when in all-white, all-beige, or all-gray space; we need contrasts for physical comfort. In fact, human beings need interiors that echo the natural spectrum as much as possible.

A dangerously monochromatic environment like this office can be improved but not totally fixed. Contrasts, both light and dark, must be carefully chosen and introduced. Naturally, their location affects the outcome. The designer must have an understanding not only of a particular item but also its relationship to the items around it. A space can be made to seem more human by adding softer textures. Individual control should be made available as much as possible but in a way that doesn't interfere with the operation of the building as a whole.

It's not simply the choice of color that's important, but the shades, textures, location, and the way light hits the different surfaces. Today there is scientific evidence as to which colors are right for which items. Color is a serious science.

Lighthouse International, a non-profit organization dedicated to providing vision services, has come up with new guidelines for effective color contrasts for people with low vision. Dark colors from the spectral extremes should be paired with light colors from the mid-spectrum.

ADA accessibility guidelines state that the key to enhance color discrimination is to maximize luminance contrast, measured as the difference between intensities of light reflected from the foreground and background of a pattern.

Good taste is not enough. Design is successful and worthy of being called good design only when it answers the needs of the people who live and work in a space, and is pleasant to look at as well. Today we can do so much to make environments suitable to their functions because we have better and more in-depth information.

RESPONSIBILITY TO KEEP LEARNING

Interior designers who haven't updated and refreshed their learning are just as lax and potentially dangerous as doctors who left medical school in 1980 and haven't cracked a book or attended a seminar since. Fortunately, doctors are forced to take continuing education, but, as we know, some are more diligent than others. In our case, not updating learning is morally wrong because the term "interior designer" carries an implied background and knowledge. When you practice with incomplete or inadequate knowledge, you're not only cheating yourself and your clients of a good result but you may also be creating a dangerous environment.

A designer who sees that the client has a low-vision problem or some physical impairment and doesn't tactfully offer design options that will improve that person's quality of life is just as dangerous to society as a medical doctor who realizes his or her patient has high blood pressure and doesn't suggest changes that will help control the problem.

It's a matter of attitude. If you knew that tomorrow you were going to perform cutting-edge work that meant life or death to someone, you'd brush up on your techniques, call people who had done that procedure, and review the details of the procedure. If you expected to be doing the same thing tomorrow that you've done for sixty-two years, and it's no more engrossing than sweeping a floor, what's the point of refining your techniques?

I see "designer" and "leader" as synonymous. If you're a leader, you have a responsibility. You have a responsibility to the person who can't keep up—whether that person has low vision, mobility problems, or some other idiosyncrasy. Even if the people you're leading are more capable, your responsibility is to help them develop within the range of their capabilities.

Interior designers are educators as well as leaders. As educators, we must realize that we can improve the way society lives. We can't blame society's problems on the police force, the government, or anyone else. We have to examine our roles. If design is an influential element in our lives—I think it is, and human-factors research supports this idea—then individual designers have perhaps more power to change things than almost any other profession.

Doing nothing is immoral. It's sinful, in a sense, because we have knowledge. We know we can improve environments, and in doing so, the quality of people's lives. Changing behavior through interior design is constructive and peaceful. In doing our jobs properly, we're improving environments and causing no harm. But if we don't take the proper actions, we are often creating harm. No, we're not going out and shooting people, but we may be doing worse things without realizing it. In designing environments that are inappropriate for the way people live, through neglect of physical or safety issues, psychological issues, or even cultural mores, how many lives are we destroying?

Design is a cultural development tool, and we must use it. Interior designers shouldn't wait to respond as victims. We should try to direct or design as leaders.

DESIGNERS AS AGENTS OF CHANGE

Business is the engine of modern society and will play a dominant role in shaping the future. This makes business people responsible for the quality of our future, as Rinaldo S. Brutoco, founder of the World Business Academy, said in a forum sponsored by the Academy. They must act as trustees for human society.

Many countries have stronger links through business than through politics. When business, medical, and other professional groups speak to each other, they get along fine, even if political leaders are still arguing. The businesses get along because there is a certain basic understanding within a discipline. Coming together for business purposes gives people from many countries the opportunity to experience different ways of life. It helps shape their new directions. Contact is important. It changes faceless countries into countries full of people, and people make changes.

Today our government is trying to change the world. In many cases, we wonder if it's working. We see major changes within different businesses that are just amazing. It's a shame the press does not put as much emphasis on this as it does on government conflicts.

Let me take this one step further. As I have stated throughout this book, I believe interior design shapes human behavior. Communication is even affected by the placement of chairs, which can influence the way people interact with each other. I think interior designers should acknowledge that their field shapes human behavior, and people in business shape the world. Together we can do great things. We are the engineers. We are the leaders. We are the designers of tomorrow. Rather than just responding to the requests of our clients, we should demonstrate that interior design is a powerful element in the process of change.

The future of our field lies in identifying a mission and linking resources and designers to achieve this mission. Interior design can show people how to deal more effectively with each other through the effective design of space. We could almost make a religion of it. The interior design field could be a Mother Theresa for the environment.

There can be no happiness if the things
we believe in are different from the
things we do.

—FREYA STARK

There is a story about a highly successful American businesswoman who felt her life was not fulfilling. She wrote to Mother Theresa, asking if she could join her mission in Calcutta. Months went by. Finally, Mother Theresa responded with a letter one sentence long: "Thank you very much for your interest, but find your own Calcutta."

Interior design has its own Calcutta right here. Changing behavior by changing the quality of the environment is a goal broad enough in scope to keep us all busy, and challenging enough to be worthy of our interest and creativity.

From my experience with the Milton Hershey School and every other project in my career, I've come to the conclusion that designers are responsible for directing behavior. We need to take this responsibility seriously.

MISSION STATEMENTS

We hear a lot about mission statements these days. A mission is a very clearly defined direction or focus. It's an accomplishable goal. There is an end point, and there are benchmarks to reach in accomplishing that goal. By defining the objectives of your practice, you establish your orientation and your focus—what is valuable to you.

The mission statement at my firm is to provide the best possible service to our clients and to enhance their lives to the greatest extent attainable through interior design. We want to keep our clients for life, and we want to be part of their development.

What the home furnishings and design industry really needs is a mission statement. This is a service industry, so the mission statement should focus on how the industry can best meet the needs of our customers.

A great design industry is composed of talented people and resources dedicated to using the scientific and artistic tools of design to enhance the way our clients live and work.

Thoughts for the Design Community

- The client and project come first.
- The design group as a whole deserves your loyalty, respect, and trust. Dedicate yourself to the group.
- Encourage everyone in the group to be a master of his or her discipline.
- Learning should be a goal and pleasure for everyone.
- Each person should be trained in leadership, treated as a leader, and expected to lead when he or she has knowledge or insights others lack.
- Speak about and deal with the project in real terms. Don't whitewash or oversimplify, even to yourself.
- The world constantly changes. We want more than just change. We want to grow with the process.
- Each short-term activity has long-term consequences. A system puts short-term activities into context; we need systems with which to approach our business.

Notes

1. Sherrill Whiton. *The Elements of Interior Decoration*. New York: Lippincott, 1944.
2. Edward T. Hall. *The Hidden Dimension*. New York: Doubleday-Anchor, 1966.
3. Robert Sommer. *Personal Space: The Behavioral Basis of Design*. Englewood Cliffs, NJ: Spectrum Books, 1969.
4. John Pile. *Interior Design*. New York: Abrams, 1988.
5. Leslie Kane Weisman. *Discrimination by Design: A Feminist Critique of the Man-Made Environment*. Champaign: University of Illinois Press, 1992.

CHAPTER 9

SYSTEM OF THINKING

If we do not grasp change by the hand, it
will grasp us by the throat.

—WINSTON CHURCHILL

Currently, our world is changing ten times faster than it was fifty years ago. If we think of everything that's changing in every area of our lives, we realize we're dealing with a whirlwind of change on a daily basis.

Items that were expensive and considered important at one point, such as calculators, are now available in miniature pocket sizes, which are more efficient and useful. They cost a fraction of previous larger models. It's amazing to see the convenience of things today. Just look at your office. Consider the way we fax and e-mail. We can take a laser-based tool and measure a space without actually using a measuring tape and have the measurements be absolutely accurate. Whether it's the amount of lumens that illuminate a tabletop or the sight lines within an interior space, we can obtain information through technology.

There is a downside though. Because some tasks can be done very quickly by technology, some of our clients believe that the entire job can be completed immediately. This creates unreasonable expectations. But often our systems may be more complex today, making those expectations unrealistic. We may be able to e-mail something to an architect with great accuracy, but that architect still has to review what we e-mailed with exceptional care to be sure the information sent is correct. Moreover, with so much information, we have to be very careful to look at the particulars critical to the issue at hand and not be distracted by all the other input. We see this conflict of new and old expectations and ways of doing things constantly. We realize that all the things we were comfortable with because of the way they worked no longer work the same way.

CHANGE

In revising the fourth edition of *The Interior Design Business Handbook*, only three-and-a-half years after the third edition, I was amazed to find that only one paragraph out of twenty-one pages about banking remained relevant. The changes in banking were occurring on a regular basis. We all dealt with them and became accustomed to them. But I had no idea how much the field had changed until I sat down and looked at what banking was like three-and-a-half years earlier.

The banking industry changed one step at a time, and we adapted. The interior design industry needs to do the same thing. Today we need a structure that permits interior design to go forward. We define things the way we understood them to be previously. This gives us a tunnel vision we can no longer afford. The world is changing too rapidly. The interior design industry has to change to deal with the massive and revolutionary changes of the recent past. We must change our design methods and focus.

Today, interior design is more complex than it was a few years ago, and greatly different than it was thirty-five years ago. Years ago, many furniture stores and dealerships handled all the details, from securing products to the delivery of the products. They also were responsible for whatever service issues were required. This service is no longer available today in most areas, which throws the responsibility on interior designers. They need to offer clients an extensive array of services. Clients also expect us to be able to deliver merchandise from all over the world. Today designers must be aware of the changing lifestyle issues of a shifting client base, versed in current technology, and expert in communication. This is a great challenge and a great responsibility.

Seeking Solutions

Clients expect solutions. They expect answers to their individual design problems, and they expect designers to have the resources to be able to solve them. We must know how to handle casual design dilemmas as well as very complex ones. Often, these are issues no design firm can handle alone. But the client still expects us to link them to solutions, consultants, and methods. They come to us and expect the whole matter to be resolved, whether the problem is simple or difficult.

In the field of psychology, therapy is solution-based and less psychoanalysis-focused than it used to be. Psychologists believe that what caused a problem is less important than working out a solution. In our industry, we have to know if the present process is good enough to improve. If not, should it be replaced with a new process? We have to design a solution—a new way to work—and make it happen.

How do we find solutions? We need to know the rules and how and when to break them. Today we assume that specialization is necessary. But does the client need specialists? If the client just wants to paint a wall, does he or she need a full analysis? How much of the existing system can we eliminate and still have an effective structure?

We're looking at forming teams of different specialists who can attack a problem and find the solution effectively, not through the traditional chain of command. This team is made up of knowledgeable people, each of whom is capable of making informed decisions. Technology has given us a shared information base.

In his *New York Times* article, "Marching with a Mouse," Thomas L. Friedman points out that if you do your homework, have your facts correct, and merit on your side, you can build a consistent forum for your ideas through the Internet. Small groups are able to go online, with little investment, and change major issues in the world.[1] The Internet has created an age of transparency. Everyone can learn about your company or field and can understand exactly what you are doing—and not necessarily what you're saying.

Friedman points out that the Internet can create an irresistible tide for change. This is very different than the past, when people made huge investments in marketing and promoting things they may or may not have represented accurately. Today, everything must be correct because people will find out quickly if something isn't right.

Technology

Many design products—including furniture, lighting fixtures, and others—are designed, engineered, and manufactured by computer-aided manufacturing (CAM). With this type of technology, designers and engineers are able to work with factories in other parts of the world. CAM allows many contributors to work on the same design at the same time. It eliminates endless rounds of review meetings. Through CAM technology, manufacturers can link their production process with designers and engineers.

Technology can link people together, and it can also enable a single person to do much more than one used to be able to do alone. For people who are not mathematically inclined, sophisticated accounting is possible with a simple PC and appropriate software. Today, businesses are reorganizing and restructuring their systems with technology, rather than organizing the businesses around a specific task. For example, at one point we had a bookkeeping department—a prerequisite then for almost every design firm. Technology has permitted designers themselves to input information, which then becomes part of the bookkeeping record. This doesn't require an entire department. The same is true with CAD work. As previously mentioned, firms once had CAD departments, but today, this work is done by individual designers.

However, we can't simply look at technology and marvel at what it can achieve. People computerize existing bookkeeping systems, but these systems may not fit the way they do business now. They could end up tracking useless information.

The objective isn't simply restructuring or downsizing, it's doing more with less. Reorganization requires us to look at the processes of the entire business structure to determine what works best. Maybe you need different equipment. A firm can't simply reorganize what it has; it has to look at new technology and opportunities to see how they apply to what the firm wants.

In many cases, a lot of old equipment needs to be replaced and a lot of processes need to be reviewed and revised.

We must use technology creatively. A basic PC and an Internet connection give us access to all sorts of information and resources. In general administrative matters, technology often means being able to do more with greater accuracy and fewer people. There's less need for people who do nothing but data entry; instead, each worker contributes to the team's decisions and changes.

We don't need as many checks and controls as before. Technology does the checking for us. With manual spreadsheets, if you made one mistake or changed one thing in one column and didn't in another, the whole thing was thrown off. Computer programs make all the changes for us. They're automatic and fast, and there are fewer errors. Although someone has to make sure the overall results are correct, we don't have to check every single detail the way we did before. We get a high-quality product with assured consistency.

Why Do We Do What We Do?

We're looking at performing our processes according to a natural flow, rather than basing our actions on a chain of command, documentation, or past performance.

Is there a duplication of effort? Because so much is done on the computer, certain hand processes are no longer necessary.

Let's look at how we can produce the best quality work at the most effective price. A process may have many different versions, which means you can do something one way and I can do it another way. It doesn't matter, as long as we get the desired result.

Some projects need different sources and supervision than others. For example, if we know our vendors and have worked with them many times in the past, we have developed standard ways of working and no longer need to spell out details.

Design a project as if one person could do the whole thing. Then see which parts can be done by other team members, and which by technology. Use people who are trained to do many different things, not just one specialized task. They're in a position to really understand the total job and should be able to bring more to it than a piece worker on a production line. Every member of the team should be trained and educated in multiple processes.

The job site can be anywhere. We aren't tied to one spot because of the need for equipment: office equipment is portable. Our consultants and information sources can be anywhere in the world. Technology makes communication possible in a matter of seconds. We can operate equally well in a large city or a small town.

When it makes more sense to perform a certain function on the job site than in the office, it's technologically possible to take the equipment to the job. Moving the "office" to the construction site changes the nature of the work and ties it directly to the people in the field.

One architect handled medium-sized projects from his office in a van. He was able to drive his office up to the project, see the problems, and speak with the contractors. Without leaving the site, he could complete the change orders and revise the prints. When the architect left the site, it was to go to a new job, not to run back to the office and attend to details.

Educating the Client and Excelling at Business

A single person can control a project and act as the contact between the client and design team. This person makes sure all the components are included and work together, assimilates information from a number of sources, and communicates with clients in language they can understand.

Designers have the responsibility to coordinate a total design project, including its architectural and engineering aspects. The designer-manager may use specialists who are in different offices or even in different cities. We can have a world-renowned specialist on our team, even if he or she is on the other side of the globe and never visits the site. Technology permits us to work very accurately and precisely to produce high-quality work with top-quality materials. There's no need to guess at anything because we have instant access to experts. We're living in a very litigious time, yet some of the risks are actually smaller because of our access to excellent resources. Documentation and confirmation are faster, easier, and less expensive.

Clients need designers to keep close reins on a project so that everything is coordinated. The average home doesn't contain much that's different from what was available fifty years ago. For example, most kitchens still contain a refrigerator, a sink, and a stove. However, technological enhancements of these products create dramatic changes in the way we live.

We also have more demanding clients than ever before. Peoples' needs as well as their wants are affected by their understanding of what is possible. If we show them how many options are out there, they'll want to take advantage of them.

We must find ways to educate and excite clients with the possibilities of great design. Once we show our clients what's available, the business prospects for the field will change.

The most successful practices are the ones that excel at internal management. They understand what they're good at and concentrate on it. They don't try to be "average" at everything, but are excellent at one, two, or three special areas. The important considerations to keep in mind are: who are your customers, what do they want, and how do they want you to present it? When we understand these considerations, we can work at developing our firms in the right direction. It's amazing to see designers worrying about their systems of charging without looking at what their clients are really interested in buying at that particular time. As our clients change, so must our practices.

Design teams should do things in exceptional ways so their clients can see that there's a major difference between what designers are able to do and what the average consumer market offers. We need to help them see what the interior design profession can accomplish for and with them.

REDESIGN FROM THE ROOTS UP

We shape our buildings; thereafter,
they shape us.

—WINSTON CHURCHILL

In redesigning buildings, we often have to start from scratch because the new functions of the buildings are sufficiently different from those of the previous owners. The project must be treated as an original design, even though we may use parts of the previous construction and it is technically adaptive reuse. We still work as if this was an original project to determine how that reuse fits into the building.

This is what we need to do with our design firms and with our industry. To determine the direction of change, we need to know our strengths and weaknesses, individually and as a firm.

The interior design industry is in an "elephant dance" situation. James A. Belasco, in *Teaching the Elephant to Dance*, wrote that elephants are trained by chaining them when they're young, so they can walk only a short distance.[2] When the elephants are older, the chain is symbolic, not attached to anything. The elephants have been conditioned to walk only a certain distance when they feel the chain. However, if an elephant is in a barn that catches on fire, fear will break the conditioning and allow the elephant to save itself by running out of the barn. Many people feel tied to a traditional structure. Belasco is telling us that we need to set a metaphorical fire and create "fear" to empower people within our industry to change.

This opportunity for change is really very positive. We won't have to worry about burnout because we'll be doing things differently. People burn out from doing things they aren't skilled at, not from doing what they've been trained for. Designing change is something we're good at. We should enjoy the challenge of redesigning our industry.

We have to look at the characteristics of design businesses. Most interior designers are self-reliant individuals willing to put in a lot of effort when they believe in the results. We also like change.

First we have to understand where we're going and just what we need to do to get there. We have to use our talents and our ingenuity.

Why Aren't We More Flexible?

Many design firms have their systems and aren't as flexible as they need to be. This lack of flexibility and the inefficiency of the division of labor process usually mean that many firms just aren't making enough money. We need to ask why each step and process is being done because some of them may be wrong or unnecessary. For example, in many situations, a single software package could be used to replace four, five, or even six steps in the management process of a design firm. Maybe a few of those steps are really needed to stay in place for the security of the job, but others could be eliminated or done differently.

The administrative structure for many projects is so expensive and time consuming. If we could spend our time on the actual project and leave the paperwork alone, projects would go more quickly and be far less expensive for our clients.

Why are so many design companies rigid, sluggish, clumsy, and noncompetitive? Why aren't they as creative as they could to be? A lot of us are overloaded with processes that could be handled better by a computer rather than a designer. You don't have to spend your life chasing paper.

When you redesign your business, keep three driving forces in mind.

1. Clients are key. They're the reason for our practice. Clients can be demanding, but we need to continue to develop and nurture them.
2. There's a great deal of competition in our field. It's intense, and comes at us from many different directions.
3. You can count on change. Things are changing so rapidly that if we don't focus on a target, a mission, or a goal, we can get lost.

Life Cycles and Issues That Affect Them

Before we can speak about creating a process for running a business, we need a general philosophy, a vision, and a mission. This is the strategy of the business, based on the type of business, its directions, and its objectives. Otherwise, there's no point in talking about a system. As times change, our strategies need to change as well.

A good business:

- Has the ability to grow
- Creates opportunities for reasonable profit
- Presents creative challenges
- Has the opportunity for diversification and change

Are you in the right business? My business has changed considerably. My clients have changed and the things I am able to do have changed because different products are available. The umbrella term "interior design" describes many different businesses and many different levels of involvement. Design training is used in interior design, product design, facilities work, and selling products, to name a few applications.

Businesses have life cycles.

During the introductory phase, you're thinking of strategy and how it will work. During growth, you may sacrifice immediate rewards for greater rewards in the future. Sometimes this means taking all of the profits and energy and applying them to further growth.

A business is said to have reached maturity when it's working well and profits are up. Everything is working beautifully.

Decline is a normal part of every business. The traditional design business has been in decline. The field has developed into a much larger, more professional service business. At one time, interior designers earned a great deal of money by selling products. Now we provide more services. Those cycles may change again. We may rise through the process to the point that selling merchandise becomes much more profitable and popular again.

Some interior design businesses are seasonal. When designers work at the seashore or in a resort area, they know clients will be there only part of the year. They know what the cycles are, and they work around them. I never thought of my business as having a seasonal cycle, but a nasty winter showed me very clearly how weather affects business—not to mention our whole income and profit structure.

Cycles affect the structure of business. The products designers sell and the way we sell them have completely changed. This means we should reevaluate how selling products affects the rest of our business. What else needs adjustment?

Cycles are normal. They occur in everything from the economy and interest rates to world events such as war. There's an economic cycle. When corporations have to lay people off, they're not going to spend large amounts of money on their corporate headquarters. They have to be very conservative, and this affects the interior design business.

There's a social cycle as well. When it becomes inappropriate for people to look opulent, their spaces become very basic and conservative. In a period such as the Reagan years, it became socially acceptable for people to have well-appointed homes and lavish clothing. That was good for the design industry. In the past few years, we've seen an opulent period in which individuals are investing in extremely large homes. People are moving to homes three, four, or five times bigger than the ones they're leaving. The scale of these houses is so large that the furnishings clients had in their previous homes aren't usable.

There's also a mature market that's untapped and eager for attention. Older people aren't hesitant to invest in their environments. In many cases, their children are earning more money than they themselves had ever earned. These active seniors have decided that they're going to live, enjoy, and do what they want to do. Often they want a completely new environment. They have different design needs than families with school-age children. The way children are cared for has changed, and that affects design from residences to day-care centers.

Legal issues affect the design industry too. The ADA regulations require businesses to make buildings more accessible to a broader range of people. These regulations brought business to some design firms, both in assessing whether structural changes were necessary and in making the changes. HIPAA regulations have made major changes in facilities related to the medical field. Restrictions based on environmental issues are causing a great deal of fear and concern; interior designers now need to make sure they're not legally responsible for issues they can't control, such as the way the chemical components of furnishings interact.

We're concerned about the environment because of global warming. With the price of oil, we're now concerned about fuel consumption as well. Many of the energy-saving processes discussed many years ago were not considered important because there weren't sufficient economic reasons for the investment. Now, people are very concerned. They're requesting that their facilities be made fuel-efficient. We're designing environmentally sound houses that take less fuel to heat and are looking for ways to make larger spaces less expensive.

People don't want to live in an area where the political atmosphere is uneasy and difficult; this affects our client base. People will move to regions with fewer taxes or a better social environment.

Political issues also affect our work. Interior designers are now licensed in many states. There's also legislation to limit the activities of interior designers.

Technological advances have brought us many new products; these also affect the way we work.

All of these factors must be considered in your business strategy.

Changes in the Industry

For years, managing growth was a big issue. The problem now is the total cost of a design project. In many cases, our direct costs are down. Furniture can be produced less expensively than ever before. However, soft costs in the form of furniture distribution and running an interior design firm are up. The administrative task of tracking and controlling a project can cost more than manufacturing or constructing the product or the project itself.

We are dealing with a new set of demands to restructure our businesses, putting the effort and energy where they are needed. The people assigned to single-task jobs will need to change as their work evolves. The entire interior design industry needs to work very differently than it did in the past.

Technology changed the market for design services, and, as I wrote earlier in this chapter, it has also made task-oriented jobs obsolete. Our limits have also changed. Access to information and communication means that talented designers are no longer tied to major cities. Today, with technology and communication, you can obtain all the information you need and work anywhere. Location no longer limits you to certain types of projects.

Our staffing needs have changed. We now need people who know how to use technology, have good people skills, and are knowledgeable in more than one area.

We must ask basic questions. What should a business look like today? What should our products look like, and how are we going to make it happen? What do we have to do to create that new design?

This doesn't mean you have to throw everything you know out the window. Change is a process, and Pareto's 80/20 rule still applies. The Italian economist of the early twentieth century said that 80 percent of the income in Italy went to 20 percent of the population, but that's been extrapolated into a more general rule. We spend 80 percent of our time doing something that's 20 percent of the process and 20 percent of our time on the other 80 percent—the most valuable part.

Look at your day. What are you doing that you really need to do? What's directly related to completing a client's project? What are you doing as a matter of course that doesn't contribute to the main objective of the project? This is what we need to look at in redesigning a design firm and the entire industry. What can be eliminated? How can we change our thinking, habits, and business structures to direct our energies more effectively toward the clients and projects?

In many small companies, management and planning are not given major emphasis. These firms are worried about issues such as cash flow. Now people starting businesses need greater amounts of capital, a much stronger business structure, and links to the right resources to be effective.

Our client base is as important as our consultants. Just as we link with resources to fit our clients, interior designers are going to have to find the right clients to fit individual practices. We will be able to serve many more types of clients than we did in the past. We're also going to have to cater to those clients and keep them happy.

We used to be able to work from crisis to crisis without taking time to consider where we were and where we should be. We expended a lot of energy on designs to show clients how important they were in avoiding problems. But at the same time we rarely planned for our own firms. We need to look at our firms in the same way we look at each project. We need to plan based on the situation today—the parameters of each project and the most effective way to get it completed.

Running a business is a science and an art. There's a definite structure, and there are challenges. We must meet the demands of every aspect of our business. We can't simply wait for the "project of the year" to walk in the door.

Change the Way You Think

*The will to win is important, but the will
to be prepared is vital.*

—JOE PATERNO

Strategic relationships with both clients and resources are the key to successful design projects and businesses. We must keep and maintain these relationships because they're not easily replaced. Shared experiences build a basis for communication. If a client or resource knows you well, the level of trust and of design will grow with each project.

Designers who cultivate relationships have practices built on what seems to be a minimal number of strong clients. One designer friend's practice has been based on three major clients for over thirty years. It's a terrific practice! He has done a lot to take care of these clients, and it has been worth his while.

We must change how we think as well as what we do. We must replace old practices with new ones. In *The Winner Within*,[3] Pat Riley says leadership means defining reality. We define reality for clients. They have all these grand ideas, and we come in and say, "This is what you can do, and this is what you can't do. This is how it can be done." Many times we walk out of a project because the goals and objectives of the client are so different from what we can actually accomplish.

Preparation and Research

Interior design is going to take a lot more preparation and research than ever before. It already does. Clients expect to hear all the details; they're no longer satisfied being told, "Everything is going to be just fine." We need to back up our judgments with documented and detailed information. This is what people are used to today. They expect background data, information, and statistics to be available whenever they ask for them.

VALUES

Words such as "value," "ethics," and "judgment" can be confusing because everyone defines them differently.

If the value of a company is the sum of all the values it teaches, thinks, and practices, there's no room for highly individual definitions. All members of a firm should be operating from a very similar set of values. If you lead a firm, clarify your definitions and share them with the other members.

"Mediocrity . . . is inevitable if the leadership of the organization perceives integrity as something that can be compromised rather than as a guide to help lift and pull the organization toward the future," Joe Batten wrote in an article in *Management Review*.[4] Batten is a leadership consultant who has written more than fifteen books on the subject.

Quality is a value. Customers want it; we want to produce it. A management strategy based on it is Total Quality Management (TQM). Batten says effective TQM demands a Total Quality Culture, "the never-ending quest for greater quality and service in every dimension of the organization. It encompasses the philosophy, central values, and practices of an organization and involves all its people and resources."[4]

Quality depends on people. People turn a vision into a reality. Each person who contributes to a project affects its success.

You can't assume your values are your clients' values. You must either redefine value for them by educating them throughout the project or accept their values as the standard for the project. Combining these two methods is more likely to produce positive results than either one alone.

Our values have changed because our clients' values have changed. A lot of merchandise once available only to designers can now be obtained by almost everyone. But clients still want the magic. They want interior designers to use their magical ability to do something far beyond what they could do themselves. Clients expect us to use our design creativity to the maximum. They don't want a repetition of things they see elsewhere; they want something customized to suit them. This forces designers to work more creatively.

ETHICS

People speak about ethics as if they were a threat. There's so much fear that it gets in the way. But there's nothing frightening about ethics. In interior design, in business, and in life, an action is ethical when it benefits everyone involved. Business schools teach ethics as a sort of moral absolutism: do the right thing simply because it is right, even if it means your company going under. A lot of people avoid the issue of ethics entirely because a black-and-white moral standard is often unrealistic. It takes years to build a productive business and a good client base. Why throw everything you have built out the window for a principle you only partly understand? We don't want to jeopardize our practice by doing anything unprofessional or unethical. But the standards are changing. Certain issues become dominant at given times, not because of what's happening in the interior design field but because of changes in our general social structure.

To define interior design ethics, we have to clearly define our profession, our specialties, and the process by which we make interior design happen. Ethics are based on good business practices. Business practice is the system for coordinating interactions between clients and design sources.

In an ethical situation, clients receive a project of value in exchange for their investment. Designers are appropriately compensated for their efforts, whether the compensation is money, publicity, or other forms of payment. The sources—contractors and various vendors—receive adequate compensation for the quality of their labor and merchandise. Ethics includes a respect for all the participants in a project.

It's our responsibility to see that our firms earn an appropriate income. We must also see that our employees are properly compensated and that they have the right tools to work with—whether the tools are equipment or training. These are our ethical responsibilities.

There's no point in a designer becoming a martyr and giving clients something for nothing just because that makes the designer a better person. Even better people have to eat.

The financial part of our business is an evaluation tool. Our clients determine how much they want to invest in a project. We use money to pay our staff and sources and to cover the overhead costs of doing these projects.

Ethics are basic business principles of respectful communication. We build relationships with clients from the first contact through interviews and decision-making. We develop a rapport with our resources—learning about their skills, ability to produce, and the capacity of their factories. We study the products to learn the scope of appropriate use. Then we evaluate the match between the products and resources and the client's circumstances, needs, and budget.

Thousands of elements can affect our decisions: performance levels, artistic value, appropriateness for the space. As much as we may like a design, it may not be possible. What good is a beautiful product if it's too expensive or simply can't be installed?

As designers, we're responsible for reviewing clients' human dimensions—being aware of more than they tell us in words. Take note of how clients act and move, how well they see and hear, and how they respond to tactile sensations. Some people dislike rough or nubby textures. A person who wears glasses or contact lenses will, at some point, remove them and perform certain tasks without them. A person who drags his or her feet because of a physical limitation is very likely to trip on the edge of that beautiful oriental rug. Design should allow for these human factors.

It's the designer's responsibility not to kill too many people with our designs. We must look at our projects critically to ensure that nothing will injure the people who must use the spaces. This includes children, older people, visitors unfamiliar with the spaces, people in a hurry, and those who are not quite awake.

It's our responsibility to remain up to date in all areas of design requirements, from codes and laws to trends. Our clients don't want the same products that can be found in the local department store or Ikea. They want products specifically chosen for their needs. This may mean custom-designed pieces, or it may simply mean using catalog items in new and different ways.

In interior design we become involved in many aspects of our clients' private lives, whether we're doing a business or residential project. Maintaining the boundaries between designer and client is a critical issue. Show that you are sensitive to this issue. If you feel you must open dresser drawers and count items of clothing, ask the client if you may do so, or if he or she would rather do it.

Client confidentiality holds the same obligation for interior designers as it does for physicians and attorneys. You may gain personal information that could harm a marriage. In a business situation, a designer may become part of a plan for a client's business growth. If the details were to be made public, this could damage the business, to say nothing of the designer–client relationship.

Ethics and respect for boundaries also exist between the designer and vendors. Our resources may have proprietary methods for making or finishing products. Designers may have developed their own unique ways of doing things. These proprietary techniques may be the basis of their income. There are things clients don't need to know, and there are things designers don't need to know. Clients should understand that the craftspeople working in their spaces need to concentrate on their work. Even though the spaces belong to the client during construction, they are also the craftspeople's workplaces.

Throughout the entire design process, we have to communicate and learn. If we don't have effective communication, the quality of the design and of the project will be in jeopardy, and we will all lose. When products are used incorrectly or don't perform well, our resources lose. Design firms lose too, because the perceived quality of their design is affected. That project won't generate new business. Of course the client is the big loser because he or she hasn't received the very best that could be produced.

For some people good communication is impossible; there's a strong likelihood for fatal misunderstandings in working with such people. In my experience, there are no lawsuits when there is good communication. It's the designer's ethical responsibility not to take on a client with whom he or she cannot communicate well or to discontinue service after becoming aware of a poor match.

In the end, ethics are just common courtesy and sound business practice. Author Robert Fuighum's claim that he learned everything he needed to know in kindergarten (in the book so named) has a lot of truth to it. Play fair, share everything, don't hit people, clean up your own messes, and say you're sorry when you hurt someone. That's ethics.

Ethical Purpose

Businesses must have a purpose beyond the bottom line. It has become the style to have commandments. In the interior design field, the commandments are:

- To give quality service to our clients beyond their expectations. To bring them all the products and services required for their projects.

- To give our clients value. Make sure they get the best possible job for their investment.
- To bring home a reasonable profit to pay for our resources and compensate our employees appropriately.

We can't earn our entire income from a single project. We need standards for charging that are fair and simple. It isn't ethical to charge more because you believe the client won't know the difference. I want to give my clients the best project I can for the best possible dollar amount. I know that to keep clients over the long term, I have to offer them quality and honest service. When we manage to save money on items, we pass along the savings to the client.

Our firm's mission statement is to provide the best design service to our clients and give them the opportunity to enhance their lives to the highest level that can be achieved through design. We want to keep our clients for life, and we want to help them find fulfillment in life.

Johnson & Johnson's credo is famous. They provide:

- Service to customers
- Service to employees and management
- Service to the community
- Service to stockholders

This is why Johnson & Johnson responded to a rash of product tampering that resulted in deaths by recalling the product. The company devised more tamper-proof seals and embarked on a public relations campaign that stressed the reliability of the product. The firm saw no other possible way to react because of its ethical standards. Experts had predicted that the brand was dead based on the loss of trust the deaths had inspired. The public responded with what marketing experts at the time called a miracle.

RESPONSIBILITY

Interior designers have to assume much more responsibility on projects. It goes against legal advice to limit design liability. But designers who get work and continue to get work are those who are truly responsible for their projects. Today people are willing to pay for assured results. They don't want to buy something that has loopholes or "ifs and buts."

Each period brings with it different responsibilities. Today's clients want the designer to be responsible for the total job, even though they want to be part of the decision-making process. Most clients know enough about interior design to realize the potential for bad decisions. They often can't complete a project easily with the level of skill and knowledge of product-quality they possess, and they know it. They recognize that working with a designer will expand their range of choices and increase the quality of the final product. Clients want designers to make the environment they dream of a reality.

Assuming responsibility while limiting risk means accepting projects you know your firm can bring to a successful conclusion. This is an important consideration in selecting new projects. Don't do it unless you're sure that you can complete the project with reasonable ease and without being overly concerned about liability issues. There is no such thing as a contract that will truly protect you from problems or from being sued. The only real protection is experience and confidence in an extended team of vendors and contractors.

Contracts are necessary. They're as important to our system as bonds and certificates of insurance. Contracts are a part of clear communication, but they can't protect us from choosing the wrong client or the wrong product. They can't protect us from a breakdown in the designer–client relationship, which is the real reason designers get sued. If you're so afraid that you feel you need contracts spelling out who is responsible for what to protect you, probably this isn't the right project or client for you.

Manny Steinfeld, founder and longtime president of Shelby Williams, said that there are very few lawsuits against a designer or manufacturer in the United States that the designer or manufacturer ever wins in court. So choose clients with whom conflict is unlikely.

Accounting for your results and assuming responsibility are at the core of Total Quality Management, employee empowerment, customer service, and most other popular tools in business management. Nothing will work as well as it should if people won't accept personal responsibility for their own actions.

In his book *The Oz Principle,* Craig Hickman sets forth four basic principles for constructive change.[5] The first is to recognize reality for what it is. Next, own it. You may not have created the problem, but you are part of it. Accept it, and go on from there. Solving the situation is the third step. Instead of saying "Why me?" just go on and plan your solution. Finally, do it. Put your plan into action.

The responsibility for handling a design project should rest with the designer. Working with vendors and craftspeople whose quality of work you know decreases your actual risk. When you share a project with other very knowledgeable consultants and vendors, you also share the responsibilities with them. Clients expect us to put together a team of resources. They want us to select contractors and vendors who understand the expectations of the project and exactly what's needed. Today's world is such that if we don't work together, it becomes too expensive and almost impossible to do a quality design job. The adversarial relationship that used to exist—and was accepted and even expected among designers, contractors, and vendors—isn't acceptable anymore. Clients don't want to hear why something didn't work. They want to know what you're going to do to make it right.

A company must have a consistent core of key players and be flexible enough to work with varied consultants specific to a project. These high level individuals aren't necessarily on our regular payroll but are still a part of our team. Communications technology enables us to consult with experts who may never actually visit the site of a project.

Know your vendors and craftspeople. Security and safety are major concerns. It's our responsibility to monitor the people we send into each project. We read stories about other businesses where staff turn out to have criminal records. How much do you know about the background of the carpet layers, electricians, and other vendors working with you on projects? This is an area in which we must be very cautious.

JUDGMENT

Good judgment is an essential tool for designers to have and to nourish. We use our judgment to sift through the many sources of products and information to design a project. It creates an awareness of the context of a project that allows us to make accurate evaluations and interpretations and to see the bigger picture

Judgment may involve the critical evaluation of a person, product, space, or situation. It means matching available products to our clients' needs, values, and directions. It also includes the process of appreciation, comparison, and appraisal of values—often expressed in attitude. Good judgment involves an accurate awareness of the meaning of cues and stimuli. It requires a designer to discriminate, weigh risks and benefits, and anticipate events to make an accurate appraisal.

Poor judgment leads to a misreading of the cues, which results in an unwanted outcome. If a person is unable to weigh the impact of an event, he or she is likely to show poor judgment. Poor judgment can negatively affect every item in the room.

There is definitely an element of intuition in good judgment.

VISION AND PURPOSE

Most adults have goals and objectives but little sense of vision. Vision is a specific destination, a picture of a desired future. Vision without purpose has little value.

We all have vision. It's what we do with it that's important. Creative people use vision, teamed with reality, to bring about change.

Vision establishes direction. Purpose is the reason an organization exists. This includes short- and long-term objectives, but purpose reflects the core values of the organization.

One purpose of a design firm might be to design great interior spaces that change and develop the opportunities of our clients. Through design, we give our staff an opportunity to express and use their talents.

Vision is knowing something has to be done. There's no alternative; it just must be done. We need to build a shared vision within the home furnishings and design industry, but individuals have to develop their own visions before they can be shared.

Some people don't think of themselves as visionaries, but they may be called that nonetheless. If you can communicate your vision so other people become excited and passionate about being part of the team, you have one of the requirements of leadership.

Designers are born visionaries. We have an obsession to create. There's such a great need today for design vision. We just have to put it into a system and to be able to communicate it.

POWER

What is power? The best definition I have found is that power is the ability to get things done. That includes being able to put together the right people and resources to accomplish your goals.

Today, power results principally from relationships. Whether it's marketing, management, or leadership, everything is based on the style of relationships. The strongest companies are built on whom you know and whether you can match the right person with the right project.

Being a good architect of time is an example of power. Planning time is just as important as planning space. It requires just as much input and just as much thought. It can shape the way we do business, just as environments affect the way we behave. Create a time system that works and helps you, or you'll be constantly fighting time.

Information is power. Being able to locate the right information is a demonstration of power. It doesn't matter if that information comes from vendors, consultants, craftspeople, networked resources, your library, the Internet, the encyclopedia, or whatever you have at your disposal that builds your base of information. Harvard professor of business administration Howard H. Stevenson says, "To be powerful, you must be able to compute your value in the marketplace you want to conquer, change the estimate that market places on your value, and convince that market of the value of your assets, services, or products."[6]

Power comes from understanding your range of knowledge and working within it. You can expand what you know, but you should work within the realm of what you already know. One can be a generalist in life, but professionally, interior designers must be specialists. The field has become so

129

complex that no single person can claim to know all there is to know.

You may have exposure to the law as it applies to interior design. But as a designer, you wouldn't practice interior design law unless you had a law degree. We may have a basic understanding of many design specialties—teleconferencing, interior plantscaping, or construction management, for instance—because we have worked with those specialists on several occasions. But that doesn't substitute for training and experience. It would be unprofessional, almost dishonest, to claim that a single person or small firm can handle everything in a house. Do a reality check on your firm. Who are you, what do you know, and what can you design?

Focus is the most important discipline. Look at the star performers in interior design and other fields. These "stars" focus on the needs of the time and the needs of their clients, and then they devise ways to meet those needs.

Designers are visionaries, but power is more than the ability to have vision. You have to be able to carry them out. Presenting a concept you can't produce at an acceptable level of quality erodes your professional credibility. Don't present a design you can't produce well.

On the other hand, in today's market, it's really dangerous to seem too powerful. It's the people who are most visible who get into trouble. Politicians have been absolutely destroyed by media exposure of some incident in their lives. How you use your power is important.

Maybe the outdated concept of designer as a master of the unknown has backfired and is part of the reason the industry is in chaos. Initially clients were loyal because they believed they couldn't get well-made products anywhere but through designers. Many of these products are now everywhere. But having a lot of choice can be confusing and exhausting. Designers are able to take the mass of information and show clients how to discriminate and find what they need.

Recently, a client asked me about a decision that had to be made on her project. I told her that decision could be made only after we made two other decisions. She said, "You know, I think that's the thing I appreciate most about this relationship. You put things in order, so I'm not stressing out over making mistakes."

Part of the power of designer–client relationship lies in the ability to put decision-making into a context that makes it exciting, positive, and reasonably easy for the client.

Somebody once commented that if something is really interesting, it's probably not worth much. Think of all the hours we spend talking about the idiosyncrasies of clients, designers, and life in general. It's interesting and even fascinating, but is it really important? Some products are presented with very large promotional and advertising programs, but the presentations don't give us what we need to know. We have to look at the constants—not at what's interesting or fun, but what really works.

We used to say that a person was as valuable as his or her Rolodex. Today, perhaps, we're as valuable as our Internet connection and access to information systems. Interior design is the system that enables us to bring this information and these systems to clients. You can't run a design studio without good information. You can have the most beautiful space filled with wonderful objects, but what do they represent? Are these objects what you need to complete your projects?

Do you truly understand your limitations? Your design history indicates both limitations and opportunities. This knowledge is your strength. We can use the technique of concession. We can tell clients there are some areas in which our skills are not as good as in others. Stress the strengths, but admit the limitations. This keeps you from taking on projects that will require too much learning as you go along.

The strongest designs are not always those associated with a specific style, period, or particular designer. The strongest designs arise from meeting the needs of a given situation. It's a matter of how well the designer investigated the needs of the client, and how well the results meet those needs.

Attributes of a Powerful Organization

A powerful organization doesn't have rigid, top-down management. Instead, it has a strong sense of mission all employees have been educated to share. The leaders of these organizations know how to bring a team together. They realize that without a team, you don't have anything.

Whether it's large or small, a powerful firm has good support often provided by an advisory board or a single person. An advisory board doesn't have the same responsibility as an official board of a corporation; usually, there's no liability. A board is made up of people who can help, by introducing you to the right people, or by teaching you what they know about the field. Good members of an advisory board include suppliers, the past owner of the firm, or anyone who knows you and understands the field. An advisory board is a powerful resource, on call but not constantly present.

Traditionally, a powerful person was the one who gave orders. Today a powerful person is one with the ability to orchestrate profitable change.

You can develop a powerful firm through developing your staff: you want them to experience a wealth of opportunities and of action. Arthur Gensler, who heads one of the largest interior design firms in the nation, says he has succeeded by hiring people who are smarter than he is. Hiring people who challenge you increases your strength. It makes people think you are stronger and smarter than you may actually be.

Power by intimidation is not where design challenge is today, even though intimidation seems built into power. Clients are often afraid they'll make the wrong decisions or that they don't know the right people, the right contractors, the right products. They're afraid they don't have the skills you do. Your knowledge can be intimidating.

Power, on the other hand, is concentration, meditation, and listening effectively to the people you communicate with. Power through communication can be developed through marketing. You can have great power and ability, but if no one knows about them, they won't do you any good.

Marketing is about relationships. It's courting your potential partners. Marketing is based on getting to know each other and developing clients' confidence in your abilities. This is the kind of marketing that works best for interior designers because the knowledge we gain in working with a client can be quite intimate.

Two qualities are extremely important in a capable designer. Today a top designer is a person who can create items of intellectual property, exclusive to his or her practices. Anyone can come up with one or two or even five good ideas. On the other hand, a top designer may not have the time to realize even

15 percent of what he or she designs. Second, a top designer knows how to inspire and empower people to be productive.

IMAGE

What do people think of when they hear "interior design"? Peter Senge discusses this in *The Fifth Discipline Fieldbook.*[7] Is it the image they see on television? As we discussed in chapter 6, there are so many "quick-fix" interior design programs such as *Trading Spaces* and *Design on a Dime*, which lend the impression that anyone can do interior design and can do it quickly. As I have explained, the presentation of interior design on those shows isn't intended to be the literal truth. Still, it affects the way designers work by coloring what people think of our profession. Maybe we need someone to write television scripts that are based on reality.

Today, we have to consider how we dress. Does it fit our client base and the area in which we are working? It's fascinating to see the way designers dress in different areas. Their clothes may be very attractive and appealing, but they probably wouldn't fit another environment. An extremely successful restaurant designer wears only jeans. But she wears them with great style and a touch of elegance; that's her signature.

Opulence is back in style, but it may not be the traditional three-piece suit or the plush corner office. This may not be the way leaders want to be seen. So often they want to appear to be part of the group of individuals they work with, whether in style of dress or in their work environment.

New York City Mayor Michael Bloomberg, for example, works with his whole team in one room. He has never had a private office and doesn't believe in it. Today we have a different management style in almost every field. It's affecting the way we, as designers, need to present ourselves. We have to look at our studios—their location and many other issues. Most of all, are they comfortable spaces for the work we're doing?

Our clients today are very bright. They see, they know, and they understand more than in previous years. They have been exposed to our field; as stated earlier, they may know more about some aspects of it than we do. We need to acknowledge this in every contact we have with clients. Our presentations should concede clients' knowledge and go from there.

If we present ourselves as all-knowing, we create a false image of our field. We need to be honest with ourselves and say, "This works and this doesn't, and this is why." I often tried to protect myself, my firm, and my staff by saying, "Oh, we'll take care of that, no problem." When there's a problem, it's better to acknowledge it, sometimes even to the client, and then find an appropriate way to fix it.

What's your visual image? Your letters, drawings, graphics—any visual interaction—can become dated. We need to redo our graphics every few years. The same is true for the furnishings in our studios. Some things last for a long time, but we may need different textiles or other adaptations.

Every document you send out should look professional. It represents your quality of design. Today we can format documents to give them visual appeal. We need to consider this in every document we produce.

IT'S HARD TO CHANGE YOUR SYSTEM OF THINKING

At a recent seminar I led on the changes in our business, we broke into teams to discuss the challenges in expanding a company during a period of rapid technological and social change.

One small contract design firm specializing in medical centers and hospitals saw itself as being in competition with some of the large design firms. The CEO of the company asked the group to suggest ways to make her firm more competitive.

We all agreed that the one thing she needed before she could consider moving into this larger arena was at least one more person as qualified as she. This person would have about the same level of education and experience and could, when the CEO was out doing marketing or client development work, keep everything running well back at the office.

How do you find a person like that? I asked her what her first step would be. She replied that she would put an ad in a newspaper, perhaps in one of the interior design magazines, or the ASID ICON. The ad would be for a project manager.

"Wait a minute!" I said, "Would you want to work for me or anyone here as a project manager? Of course not. Then why would you expect a person of the caliber you want, someone who's your equal, to come to work for you as a project manager?"

We convinced her that hiring a project manager was not the answer. When you add an equal to your firm, you have to think about what this kind of person would want. It's not a project manager's job. He or she would want to be your partner or co-owner—a key player. There are several ways to structure this relationship formally. The most important thing is to treat the person as an equal in responsibility and authority.

It's interesting that even when we know we have to do things differently to succeed in this rapidly changing market, we think in terms of the traditional system. It's hard to break habits. Business theories keep telling us to drop the hierarchical structure. They tell us to empower individuals to be more responsible for what they do, to hire independent people with greater skills and abilities to run our firms properly. But we still think in terms of hierarchy. We still think the old way.

In the new system of thinking, we must consider how people want to work. The question to ask is how it benefits you and the person you're considering hiring to join your firm. Maybe you should be merging two firms. Would that give you both an advantage? It's important that there be advantages for both parties.

A firm's value and potential may not be where they should because the wrong person was hired or was brought in under the wrong parameters. Whom do you want to work with? What conditions would that person want as part of the agreement? How will this work with the rest of the people who make up the firm? Is your current program one that will bring you the future you want? Are these the kind of people you want to spend your time with?

You have to be honest with clients and potential staff from the beginning. There's nothing about your company that anyone with reasonable intelligence and contacts cannot find out. There are no secrets. There was a day when the owner of a company kept the books away from everyone else, and no one knew what he or she made. That's not true today. Almost everyone knows exactly what you make. Once this knowledge is out, no one is comfortable with a firm that isn't very honest and forthright.

Changing your system of thinking takes experience after experience and constant reminders. You need to learn to visualize and develop your company with a new system of thinking. Without the right kind of thinking, you won't perform properly.

Hiring a high-level staff person is just as serious as selecting a marriage partner. A good relationship should last a very long time. We spend a lot of time with the people we work with—sometimes much more than we do with a spouse.

Notes

1. Thomas L. Friedman. "Marching With a Mouse," *New York Times*, March 16, 2007.
2. James A. Belasco. *Teaching the Elephant to Dance: Empowering Change in Your Organization.* New York: Crown, 1990.
3. Pat Riley. *The Winner Within.* New York: The Berkley Publishing Group, 1994.
4. Joe Batten. "A Total Quality Culture," *Management Review*, May 1994, p. 61.
5. Craig R. Hickman. *The Oz Principle: Getting Results Through Individual and Organizational Accountability.* Englewood Cliffs, NJ: Prentice-Hall, 1994.
6. Howard H. Stevenson and Michael Warshaw. "Power: A Harvard Expert Reveals How to Win," *Success*, June 1994, p. 36.
7. Peter M. Senge, et. al. *The Fifth Discipline Fieldbook: Strategies for Building a Learning Organization.* New York: Currency Doubleday, 1994.

CHAPTER 10

LEARNING PROGRAMS

There's a gap between interior design education and the practice of interior design. It used to take fifty years for information to become obsolete. Now it happens in less than a few months. University professors are required to spend a minimum of one day a week researching their fields. We are in the same situation. Interior designers cannot afford to spend less than one solid day a week keeping up with design issues.

KEEP ON LEARNING

Every day we need and want more knowledge. Fortunately, today there are many systems for gaining that knowledge. Some of those systems bring us excellent and supportive information. Other sources bring both our clients and us information that may not be the best and is, in some cases, even incorrect. Each practice needs a good system for gaining the right information.

Experience is a great teacher, but experience alone is not enough. We need to bring new techniques to our practices if we are to elevate the quality of our work and keep up with today's clients.

We learn by doing and by taking classes; however, teaching methods have changed drastically since some of us began our education. In the 1940s and 1950s, children were told to memorize. They were then given tests, wherein they proved how well they had memorized the lessons. Now, very often the teacher lets students explain subjects to each other and gives them opportunities to learn by doing. It's exciting to see that some of the subjects that seemed very dull to us in school are now being taught in a most exciting and fun way.

We'd like to think we have mastered our discipline, but each day we're faced with many issues that make us realize there is much more to learn. I think the more we learn, the more we realize how much there is to know. Some of the most successful people in any field are the most dedicated students.

Education cannot stop when you receive a certificate or a degree. I have always spent at least twenty hours a week educating myself by spending time with consultants, reading business and design publications, and taking short courses. The Internet has added opportunities to share and learn anytime, anywhere in the world. Our Designer's Business Forum, in which I have the responsibility to introduce new information, procedures, and processes to the group, has been a very rewarding way to learn and grow our practices. Seeing what each firm does with this information is exceptionally reinforcing.

The most successful corporations as well as design organizations are also institutions for learning. They make learning accessible to their employees through different means. They offer opportunities to mix socially with their competition so their members can learn from similar companies. These corporations realize that in order to stay ahead, they have to keep improving their staff's abilities and knowledge.

Continuing education should be part of every employment agreement. A certain amount of time and money should be dedicated to continuing education. The expense in time and money should be shared by the employer and employees. This is ideal, but the reality is different. Even in large corporations, continuing education today often is the responsibility of the individual, though the company may be very supportive financially or generous in giving time off. If designers want to continue to be a marketable commodity in the future, they have to be sure that their own education is developed, which is the reason we need consultants to assist us. We'll discuss this further at the end of the chapter.

Every industry needs to revamp its curriculum. The big auto-makers went into the universities and showed them how to design their programs so that instead of turning out traditional engineers, the universities are producing engineers who have suitable skills.[1] Other industries have done the same; they're working with the universities so that the engineering and science departments are turning out graduates whose skills are up to date and valuable to the corporations. Automakers want engineers with people skills. Dennis Pawley, founder of the Lean Learning Center at Massachusetts Institute of Technology and a former CEO of Chrysler, says that when he talks to students at MIT, he probably turns off 30 percent of them by describing the work. "But that's okay. I don't want them working for me," Pawley comments. He explains to the students what the real world is like with its many work challenges, as well as the political realm of the business and other aspects of working with people. They need to be ready for this; otherwise design is not for them.

Why We Need to Keep Learning

Handing clients prepackaged solutions doesn't work today. As I have stressed throughout this book, clients now have unprecedented access to resources. We need to be aware of what information they're seeing, but we also need to show them how to use that information and which parts of it are accurate, appropriate, and properly presented.

Learning increases our abilities. It makes us more marketable, whether to the individual client or the large corporation.

Passing certain tests or attaining certain credentials in interior design does not mean a person is actually qualified to deal with all problems. Once we become designers or head our own firms, we think we've arrived! We have not arrived. We really have to start all over again because the challenges and opportunities are new and different.

When we were in school, we could not imagine the many products and opportunities we have in our field today. Some of the information we learned is now useless, but the learning process itself is valuable. Fortunately, we were trained to deal with constant change. Every day we start all over again, but it is not a blank slate. Your knowledge base is everything that happened before today.

People learn from experience, but when you've been designing for a long time you have to ask yourself, does every day actually increase your knowledge, or have you simply repeated your first year twenty times? It's time to look at our practices and ask how many different kinds of experiences we have actually had.

So much in our industry repeats designs. There are often finishes or features that could be added to even the most traditional products. Clients want something different. They want something that fits a more current need. Often manufacturers will say, We know it works, so let's continue to make it. They're not meeting the demands of the day. True, it's a great design, but is this product really needed for this specific situation? We really have to reexamine our design efforts. Are we keeping up with the times, or using the same old things in the same old ways? If it's a traditional design project, and we want the historic references, there are still new products, finishes, and components that can enhance that tradition. Are we offering clients a top-level design? Are those in our industry willing to consider that some of the issues brought up by clients really are different from projects we've handled before and therefore require different solutions?

There are some wonderful stories in our field, including this one: Tom Frank, FASID, helped decorate windows in his father's store when he was fourteen. Working to pay for his design education, he learned plumbing, electrical work, welding, cement finishing, and carpentry. Later, when he became a designer, Tom could show the crew exactly what he wanted if there were questions about any of his instructions. Designers have learned so much through their early design experiences. Fortunately, I also had the opportunity to work in my father's business. It's amazing how often I bring some of these experiences to assist me in making decisions in my work today.

How can we know what to ask for when we have limited experience of what is possible? A period of working in a craft related to the design industry will deepen any designers understanding and make him or her a better designer. Many of our universities and design programs are encouraging designers to learn a craft so they can better appreciate what goes into creating a product. It's encouraging to see that designers really respect and know the disciplines they're working with.

Sharing Knowledge Unifies Groups

Just as we expect a global company to have the same standards and practices throughout its many factories, the complete

140

design field needs to be unified. Education is a great way to accomplish this.

Large corporations have what they call "cookbooks," which are documented recipes or patterns on which the creativity and the engineering of their products are based. Some of the older cookbooks are still pulled out for reference, even though there are many new techniques and products. The market changes so much, and we're ready to take on the new system. But it's often so valuable to have access to the way things were done.

Designers have a similar need to write down and share what we already know. This sharing of knowledge will wear away some of the barriers to communication that have made the design industry appear so fragmented to outsiders. Many large corporations call in university professors with years of experience to work with their internal experts in developing courses designed just for their companies. Our professional organizations, educational institutions, and industry resources should work together to create courses of education. This will help strengthen our ties to each other. This bonding will strengthen the industry as a whole.

For years, design firms have blamed problems within our industry on "outside enemies"—competitors responsible for taking our business away. Our major problem is within. Once we recreate our field as one in which continual mutual learning by the designer, the client, and the industry is part of the excitement, we will have an even greater field. Designers will actually accomplish the challenges that brought them into the field.

Designers Teach Clients

Coordinating and enhancing information for our clients is part of our role as designers. It is our responsibility to make sure the client—whether it's a person trying to direct community activity through a community center, the manager of a sizable business, or a person redoing a living room—understands the elements of the design.

It's also our responsibility to explain the environmental effects of interior design, whether they be physical, psychological, or cultural. We need to understand what these issues mean to our clients. For example, our clients need to understand that color choices are not random or arbitrary, based on whim or a fleeting trend. We need to convey that color looks different to a twenty-year-old than it does to someone who is sixty or seventy. Each new item you introduce changes the perception of color for every other item.

This type of information is available in medical texts as well as in essays on the effects of aging. We can supplement what we learn from texts on color for the artist with sociological and anthropological information.

We need to be sure our clients are aware of all the health and safety issues that affect them.

What Should We Know?

Interior design programs teach problem-solving processes but don't go extensively into communication skills. Today's students are learning not just to do office design, but many other types of social and privately used spaces. They are realizing the strong emphasis on the details of each of these spaces. Education today, fortunately, includes the scientific and other research aspects of interior design.

We are learning how to develop residential spaces that truly change people's lives. We are being trained to create new styles of community centers and public spaces. We are being trained to create environments that support and enhance the way people work, move, and interact. Information on how design affects peoples' emotions has been gathered by environmental psychologists. Sociologists Robert Sommer and Christopher Alexander wrote about this interaction in the 1960s and 1970s.[2] It seems to have taken a long time for the research to receive public attention but it finally has. We are being asked and required to use our talents to improve the way people live and work.

Designers do not want standard, routine work, stability, and minimal changes. We want to design meaningful changes. Interior design education teaches us that every day there will be a new problem we can turn into a new opportunity. This experience is perhaps one of the greatest assets we have in dealing with the challenges of today.

The world needs so much improvement. There are plenty of meaningful changes to be made. The challenge today is to improve the lifestyle of every person, at work, home, and in all types of social areas. This is our mission for the day.

We have the tools to improve life in ways no other profession can. We have to organize our professional efforts and move forward. We must stop looking to outsiders for answers. Our answers will come from looking at our own abilities and designing a field that meets the real needs of our clients and the world.

REDESIGNING DESIGN EDUCATION

The present continuing-education system is not enough. Our practice changes almost daily. As a designer, I need information and education in subjects that didn't exist when I first got my training. This information must come from a neutral, noncompetitive information source with high standards. Companies making products need to inform us of all the details so that we can use their products appropriately.

Education Today

A formal interior design education is a four- to five-year program in a FIDER-accredited college or university. FIDER (Foundation for Interior Design Education Research) recommends that one-third of design education be through formal education, one-third through professional organizations, and one-third through industry. Either during or immediately after the program, the design student serves a practicum (period of assigned fieldwork) or an internship with an accredited design firm. This is usually followed by beginning work as a junior designer for a professional design firm, with the junior member doing documentation, design development, drafting, and general support work for the experienced interior designer.

Practicing interior designers can get specialized training in the form of continuing education units, or CEUs, given by professional design organizations such as the American Society of Interior Designers (ASID), the International Interior Design Association (IIDA), the International Furnishings and Design Association (IFDA), and the Interior Design Society (IDS). CEUs are also offered through universities such as Harvard, UCLA, Parsons, Pratt, and many others. Some programs require on-campus time from a day to a week.

Master's degrees and Ph.D. programs include more intensive on-campus training. Some designers have returned to take undergraduate courses that were not offered when they were in school. In addition to programs that require campus time, there are online programs. I understand there are certain undergraduate programs that can be exclusively accessed online. However, it is extremely valuable in most instances to work on campus because of the social interaction and the opportunity to compare one designer's work to another. I often recommend that even if people are forced to do a lot of online work, they also should have the opportunity to do some work onsite because it is essential to their future careers.

CEUs bring education directly to the local design center or chapter level so designers don't have to take large blocks of time from their practices. But there are drawbacks. Today's CEU programs vary greatly in academic level according to the instructor. Design associations are successful at organizing and administering the programs, but there is no mechanism for evaluating either the programs or the skill levels of the other designers taking them. At design schools, however, a FIDER accreditation aims to guarantee that the design education will cover the essentials. For CEUs to be a reliable and effective way to update our education, we need a viable rating system of courses and students.

I just had the opportunity of giving a keynote address and a workshop for the International Window Coverings Expo in Washington, D.C. I was impressed at the strong interest in education among those attending. I was impressed at the number and quality of courses presented and also by the level of attendance and interaction in the group. As an instructor, I'm amazed how much I learn each time I go out to present. Regardless of our background, all designers can benefit from such educational opportunities.

Time Works Against Us

Rapid change has made the education of even recent graduates, let alone that of anyone who has been practicing for more than five years, obsolete. We need to be reeducated as we practice. For some designers, reeducation is essential because their specialty no longer exists or is no longer salable. A number of years ago, the hospitality field declined tremendously. Many of its practitioners realized that they had the basic background to design hospitals. Hospitals were becoming more hotel-like, so hospitality designers were able to move into that specialty. They had to learn new tools, but still, the move was possible. There are new regulations, advances that complement what we already know, and specialties that are unfamiliar. Most interior designers are probably somewhat behind on or uncomfortable with one or more issues that affect their practices.

Continuing education is a critical need for people in any business. We need access to new information and ideas daily, just to maintain our interest levels and our ability to create. The question is how to get that education while working in the field. Many designers are already committed to a position or to their own companies and therefore cannot take off a year or two to get advanced and specialized training. We need a more practical and economical way to acquire educational updates.

We have a glut of information, but there's no easy and accessible source to find reliable and accurate information. It appears almost a paragraph at a time, on the Internet, television, in general business newspapers, in the journals of fields allied to design, and in engineering journals. It also comes from day-to-day practice. Sometimes sifting through all the information to find what is usable is too big a job. To keep abreast of changes in the design field, interior designers presently must go to many different sources and try to coordinate all of them. Even that information doesn't hold for a length of time; it needs to be constantly updated.

Retired university professor of psychology and clinical psychologist Dr. Arnold Lazarus told me he is able to keep current in his field because he is blessed with very bright, inquisitive students who read widely, ask questions and "then get me scurrying off to find answers and sources I might never even have thought about without their input."

Lazarus further states that workshops can be expensive and time-consuming, and that he cannot rely solely on professional journals for up-to-date information because what people are willing to commit to writing "is not very illuminating." It is reasonable to assume that "illuminating" articles are equally few and far between in other professions. Interior design is no exception.

In interior design, as in other fields, often great presenters don't have pertinent information because they're not knowledgeable enough about a particular subject. At the same time, the people who really have had the relevant experience don't necessarily have the skills to communicate properly.

Fewer Opportunities for On-the-Job Training

On-the-job training is different today. Most designers don't need a support person, which was a position that new graduates used to take in order to get a foot in the door. But there is another possibility. If young designers coming out of school have great drafting and rendering skills and are excellent with technology, including CAD and internet referencing, they can often bring an expertise to the practice that is well worth paying for. New designers are being paid at much higher rates because of their professional skills. This also means every bit of contribution that they make has to be at a high level. They need to have had a good education to be able to tell the difference between appropriate and inappropriate references. To be a contributing and equally valued member of a team is a wonderful opportunity for the young professional, who can learn a tremendous amount if he or she is willing and able to be part of the process. Senior designers are willing to give them information, but they cannot afford to have people around who are not productive. This means the requirements for an entry-level designer have changed.

Design students say they learn more from actual practice than from all their classes and books. Today, they show more and more interest in learning the basics of running a business. Design educator Nick Politis said in an interview in *Contract* magazine that only half of what designers need to know is learned in the classroom; the other half is learned on the job.[3] It's important for both the design student and design education system to revise their models, or there will be many misplaced or disappointed people.

Jack Fields, head of Edward Fields Carpets, now part of TaiPing, says today's designers are taught the mechanics of design. Most people who are trained only in the mechanics of interior design have no basic concept of design. A design sense is inborn and gets developed throughout our lives. It isn't necessarily taught in design school. It takes a combination of both inborn talent and professional training to be successful in the design world today.

Suggested Solution

The study of business practices is the basis for design communication. To ensure student designers have skills that make it practical and economical for practicing professionals to take them into their studios, basic business practices must be a major part of every interior design curriculum. Business practices shouldn't simply consist of a course or two tacked onto a program. They should be the core of any design education.

In addition, a student should have some advanced or specialized training in CAD or the various codes, for instance. Because the working system is changing from a hierarchy to teamwork, design students should graduate from a program and be able to contribute specific skills to a firm.

The New Relationship Between Designers and Design School

I envision the relationship between the design school and design student as one that lasts as long as the individual's career. The school writes a maintenance contract with graduates, agreeing to provide coaching and informational support at appropriate levels of complexity. The school knows what courses the individual has completed and can design updated material to complement this knowledge and to challenge the designer.

There are times when a professional who has been practicing for ten or fifteen years might need a course that is taught today at the undergraduate level, and that is fine. There might be other times when undergraduate students, because of their previous background and interests, might be able to perform well in courses taught at the graduate level. This, too, should be available.

A college- or university-run continuing education program benefits the school by bringing in extra revenue. It benefits the field by standardizing the quality of information. The ideal school is staffed by a mixture of academics and professionals with practical experience in the field. A college- or university-run continuing education program benefits the students because the extra funds can buy the very finest laboratories and teachers. It also benefits the students by mingling current students with working professionals. The younger students get input from people with real-world experience. Returning designers get fresh outlooks about old problems from younger students. This interaction also demands that teaching materials stay current. A revised continuing education program for past graduates may mean that design schools need to hire trainers or teachers from outside the academic arena.

Some CEU programs currently offered through design organizations could transfer credits toward academic degrees without change. Others need new formats or presentation guidelines.

This program of continuing education elevates the quality of a design education. For the students, continuing education is a constant demonstration of the real world. For the postgraduates, it's a way to keep in touch with changes in the field and with the vital curiosity they had as students.

Easy-Access Education

The format of the training should be developed according to the demands of the subject and its complexity. Use the method of communication that will best present each subject. Some subjects might be dealt with in the form of a written bulletin, accompanied by audiovisual material. Others might require days or weeks in the classroom or laboratory.

These schools could also offer a group of consultants. When a student's faculty advisor or coach feels he or she needs individual attention, a consultant might be the answer. For example, a designer could call a coach: I ran into a lighting problem touched on by course X. I need some information that goes beyond what was presented. Which consultant from your list should I call?

The way a subject is taught can be customized to the way individuals learn: by seeing, by doing, or as intellectual constructs. Courses might include any combination of written material, videos, on-campus classes, and site visits. Ideally, they will create an opportunity for interaction between the most skilled practitioners and students.

The New Relationship Between the Design Industry and the Design School

I foresee design schools becoming partners with the design industry. For professionals to continue to earn a living in the field, they need the tools to make them proficient, expert, and current. These programs need to be coordinated with professional organizations for interior designers.

Why should designers do this? Because the field needs stronger, better-educated designers.

Why should design schools embark on a program that will require so many changes to the status quo? Design schools ought to produce students who perform with excellence. Schools should move with the changes in the industry. Enrollments to design schools are increasing. For educational institutions to grow, they need even more students. These institutions are really vital, but they still need to be revised or made all encompassing so they relate better to our needs.

Programs for design professionals must also be coordinated with the real needs of our clients, industry, and craftspeople. There are dozens of ways professional organizations and educational institutions can work together. Some programs might be offered at local chapter levels, while others might spawn discussion groups at the chapter level. Schools can become test laboratories for industry.

Why not test new products on trained observers—design students and developing professionals—who can give educated feedback? Today, many home furnishings products are test-marketed in the field and revised according to consumer complaints, which does nothing to elevate the reputation of the designer who specified the products.

Other Programs of Study

In addition to an institutional study program, we can learn by observing how other designers work and think. The Internet has been an incredible tool because most designers have Web sites that show their premier work and often explain their process. Many of our publications are very supportive. It's also wonderful to read biographies of designers and architects. I found the book *Charles Rennie Mackintosh: The Architectural*

Papers,[4] edited by Pamela Robertson, most interesting. It provides insights into how this very creative and artistic architect thought, with carefully chosen segments from his diary and personal work notes. I have a library full of designers' stories and their work.

Another informal study opportunity is to form a Delphi group, as set out in Ronald Gross's *The Independent Scholar's Handbook*.[5] The book has been called the "indispensable guide for the stubbornly intelligent," which describes most interior designers. Many people who have not gotten degrees or been associated with universities have followed their own courses of study, often by linking with other people.

The Delphi process brings together people who are interested in studying and reviewing a given subject. As in a networking group, there is a standard format for interaction. Each group member shares and develops information. Each member may write an essay on an aspect of the topic, mailing it to all other members. Members critique and learn from each others' work.

This book demonstrates that there are many other methods of learning within the educational process. Gross also targets mentoring programs as an effective way to further one's education. Intellectual partnerships are as vital as ever. They are a very valuable process for both the student and the teacher.

The Delphi group is one example of the different systems out there, but also the Internet and various blog sites have been very helpful in bringing people together. However, the legitimacy and accuracy of these sites varies wildly; some have professional review, some do not. The level of the program needs to be very carefully evaluated.

Elevate Design Standards

The point is that it's time to elevate our own standards for design education. It should be practical, stimulating, and pave the way for a stronger interior design field. Let's do it in an efficient, cost-effective manner that makes continuing education accessible to designers at all stages of their careers.

University study needs to offer more than just a four- or five-year program. It ought to provide a continuing dialogue, educational research, and quality consulting services for designers.

The economics of today's business environment demand that we constantly elevate our standards. We all have to work together—the design industry, educational institutions, and individual design firms.

Notes

1. Paul A. Eisenstein. "Big Three Automakers Aiming to Change Education," *Investor's Business Daily*, March 4, 1994, p. 4.
2. Robert Sommer and Christopher Alexander. *A Pattern Language: Towns, Buildings, Construction*. Oxford University Press, 1977.
3. Laura Mayer. "One on One with Nick Politis," *Contract*, December 1989, pp. 32–33.
4. Pamela Robertson, ed. *Charles Rennie Mackintosh: The Architectural Papers*. Cambridge: MIT Press, 1990.
5. Ronald Gross. *The Independent Scholar's Handbook*. Berkeley, CA: Ten Speed Press, 1993.

CHAPTER 11

COMMUNICATE

Interior designers have great power to persuade and to direct human behavior. People need to improve their lives. We have the ability to support them in their goals and missions—and we should use it. Design can change lives.

PERSUASIVE POWER OF DESIGN

The power of design can be subtle, sometimes almost imperceptible. But that power does exist and has a strong effect. Interior designers continually refine their art of persuasion by creating environments for people and then observing their reactions.

We have the tools to create environments that make a difference. Years of human factors research have given us more information than most of us could use in a lifetime. Now we must take our knowledge to an arena beyond that of clients who buy design services. Our knowledge and abilities can help ease social and cultural conflicts and deprivation.

For the most part, no one other than a designer can tell you what a designer does exactly. Let's change that. Let's aim to be seen as leaders by designing a better world.

The principal goals of our profession should be education and implementation. We have to educate our potential clients both on the power of design and the proper use of products. To communicate well, we have to be able to see through our clients' eyes. We have to accept their points of view without forgetting what we have learned through experience and education.

Personal service is just as important in the design industry as it is in any other field. We need to find the most effective ways to bring products to our clients with the appropriate support services.

PROBLEM-SOLVING

Finding out exactly what clients want is one of the greatest difficulties we have. Even clients who are customarily good communicators may find it hard to express what they want from a space and a designer. What *do* they want? When does the space work? When doesn't it work? What issues relate to this space? If there's a problem, under what circumstances does the problem occur?

Defining problems correctly is essential. Designers who have rapport with their clients and a sense of confidence in their abilities to problem-solve have a definite advantage. Do you have a simple process that helps you define problems? Are you able to design a process to fix the problems? Confidence in one another, built through repeated contacts and shared experiences, is the key.

THE DESIGNER-CLIENT RELATIONSHIP

Today the client is a respected and valued member of the design team. The acknowledgment that none of us has all the answers is part of the mutual respect that underlies a good relationship, and, in turn, a great project. Client relations are a lifetime project. You're never off-duty.

Successful designers are very involved in their communities through continuing their design services, charitable donations, public education programs, and just about any other way you can imagine. Demonstrating an in-depth involvement with a community means you have a vested interest in the development and survival of that community.

Cooperation is going to be far more important to us than ever before. Are we willing to work together toward excellence on a project that is attractive and beneficial to all the people involved? Are we willing to create with our clients? Are we able to use the synergism Buckminster Fuller talked about, to put two and two together so that it equals six?

Look at your own design practice and the friendships that have evolved from it. They grew because you developed mutual respect and a natural bond through working together. There's no market development program that can substitute for shared experiences.

A healthy designer-client relationship is essential to the future of the design business. When clients ask for information, make sure they get it as quickly as possible. Then call to make sure they received it. Personal, dedicated, quality service is what customers want from other service industries. Our industry is no different. Our goal is quality service built on relationships.

The Right Way to Ask Questions

We can learn a great deal and prevent misunderstandings in the way we ask questions. Part of developing a design project and the relationship between client and designer is finding out what each person knows and doesn't know.

To get useful information, be inquisitive and challenging. We never really know how and why things are the way they are with our clients, especially at the beginning of a relationship, so it's important to find out as much as you can. At the same time, show concern for the client. We especially can't afford to be critical in any way because we just don't know the client's circumstances. Our job is to be supportive.

Exchanging Information

Technology supports communication. There are times when communicating by e-mail, fax, or phone is best. At other times, a personal visit is the wisest choice. The combination is important. Today interior designers bring much more information and materials via technology to clients and co-workers than ever before. Technology is involved in every portion of a job, from the concept to the last detail of the finished project.

Providing information is one of the primary functions of a designer. Today that information must be visual and fast. There are times when videos are appropriate. This visual interactive experience can provide expert information and demonstrations of the way furniture works. We can personalize the videos and e-mail them to our clients, so they have this information for training purposes.

Having information at the right time is more important than its format. Recently a client wanted to know the origin of a particular flower in a floral print named "Outlander." The flower looked like a rhododendron to me, but I wasn't sure. We checked in the *Encyclopedia Britannica*. We learned the flower was a Mediterranean flower similar to the rhododendron. The explanation in the encyclopedia described a color similar to the one in the client's floral print. My client was very pleased to have a background story for a print she wanted to place in her living room. This bit of information made the room more meaningful and more personal.

In spite of the vital role technology plays, the most valuable method of communication is still eye-to-eye. We can't always accomplish this. But if it's at all possible, spend as much time as you can with your clients. This is exceptionally valuable in building a rapport with them.

The important thing is to be there for clients and keep current. I'm not sure if it's good or bad, but clients think that we should have all the answers immediately. It's important to explain to them that our work is a compilation of many people's efforts and giving them information without having all the details isn't valuable. Ask clients to leave you a message and let you know what they're interested in. When they give you this information, it's best to say you want to review it with all the different players to be sure all the areas are covered.

Communication Schedule

Even with all the high-tech information swapping, clients want a specific designer they can relate to and whom they can reach at any time. For your convenience and theirs, let them know a convenient time when you are available to return calls, say, between eight and ten in the morning. Once a week, schedule a phone conference to give each client an update on everything that's happening on his or her project. That way clients know you're on top of everything. The regular updates also permit you to organize your material and be professional when presenting it. I find that a phone call works best, rather than sending an e-mail or fax, because it is more interactive. A phone call gives the clients an opportunity to ask you questions or mention something they may want added to the project.

If you call and the person you want isn't in, be sure to leave the date you're calling and the date and time when you can be reached. Make it easy.

Proposals and Contracts

The standard boiler plate contract isn't appropriate today. Each firm must outline the general conditions under which it works. The firm should also review clients' needs and expectations in the proposal. It's advisable for firms to have standards in place, but take the time to personalize your proposal or contract so it appears as if it was created just for that client. Pick and choose among standard contract paragraphs that relate to the specific project and client.

Be careful not to promise more than you can deliver when you write proposals and contracts. In proposals, give the clients precisely the information they requested. Don't confuse the issues.

Refer to *The Interior Design Business Handbook, 4th Edition* for examples of contracts.

Charging

Professional expertise is the reason you were hired. Consider this when you write up your charges. Some design firms can complete a project in one-tenth the time it takes another firm, and more capably because of long-term experience. Clients today are very interested in what they receive for their investments.

Firms need to review their systems on an annual basis with a consultant familiar with other design firms to be sure they're charging appropriately for the market. Not only the costs but the entire process needs to be considered. The process may change considerably, depending on a firm's specialty and areas of responsibility.

SPEAKING

I'll pay more for a man's ability to speak
than for any other quality he might
possess.

—CHARLES SCHWAB, NOTED
INDUSTRIALIST

Communicating with our clients on a personal basis or in a formal speech requires certain skills. It's very important to review how we communicate, whether by telephone or in person. Tape your phone call to see how it sounds to the person on the other end.

We all try to communicate well. But we have to try harder to organize the information so clients can use and digest it. Not only can designers be overwhelmed by the details, they can overwhelm their clients.

First understand the information yourself, and be sure you really believe in what you're saying before presenting it. Today, people are so aware of what's real. If you truly believe in what you're saying, it invests your speech with more meaning. Beyond that, all you really have to do is work on techniques of speaking, presenting, and communicating. There's no point giving a speech if you don't believe in what you're saying.

When you are actually presenting a formal speech, it's important to have several listeners critique it. Provide them with an outline. Ask if you've adequately covered each item you intended to talk about. What can you do to improve your presentation? Who is your audience and what's its level of understanding of your subject? What are the audience's particular interests? Even though people may understand your subject, they may not be particularly interested in it. You must present your topic in a way that captures their attention.

Present one basic idea. Decide on a topic, and create a list of points that develop the idea.

Introductions are somewhat of a waste of time. It's fine to have something about a speaker's background in the written program, but the oral introduction should be short and to the point.

Preparing a speech means rewriting it many times. To get it right, you must organize the speech so that it's precise and yet covers everything you want to.

You can take classes in public speaking, and you can also train yourself and develop a style of delivery through rehearsal and practice with a critical audience, if possible.

Visual aids can help in making a point. However, when making a presentation in a darkened room, you lose a lot of the effects of personal interaction. Question-and-answer periods can be of great value, but they must be controlled. Think about which questions are likely to be asked, and prepare answers in advance. If a person asks a question not really related to the subject matter, don't bore the audience with an answer. Suggest that the questioner speak with you after the presentation.

When planning speeches, start with a sheet of paper. List the subject of the speech, the location, the group you'll be speaking to, and the length of the speech. List the points that are important to make this speech effective, and use the list as a guide when writing the speech.

Speaking can often work as a marketing tool. You don't have to be the person speaking to benefit. It can be valuable to bring in a skilled keynote speaker so you become the consultant who does the introduction and answers questions. That way you present yourself as a part of a team of professionals.

Presentations

Presentations are like theatrical performances; they work best when they're planned and rehearsed. Do you need photographs, slides, charts, or other visual aids? Today PowerPoint has become the standard. It's fascinating to see how designers have used PowerPoint to support projects. They're able to bring in detailed information and carry it in on a very small laptop or PDA and project it on a larger screen. PowerPoint can be most efficient and obviously so much easier than dragging around the large quantities of materials we had to in the past.

People today are used to excellent performances. We can't get away with off-the-cuff and spur-of-the-moment anymore. Presentations have to be well polished and relevant. Don't get so involved in the show that props and visual aids overwhelm your message.

Meetings

Meetings can be one of the most valuable or one of the most wasteful things we do. It's important to set a structure, so your clients know exactly what's to be accomplished during a meeting. It has become standard practice to send an agenda to a client a few days before the meeting by e-mail or fax. The agenda answers these questions:

- What do you expect to cover at the meeting?
- Who will be attending?
- What are their individual responsibilities?
- What information should the client bring to the meeting?
- What decisions should be made by the end of the meeting?

After the meeting, list the specific points or decisions that were covered. Send this list to the client as a confirmation. Ask the client to add any relevant points you may have left out. Do this even if the meeting was over the phone. This documentation not only reassures the client of your professionalism but provides backup in the case of future misunderstandings.

Detailing a meeting is important because it summarizes what was done and helps people understand what they will be doing next. We often go off on tangents. It's important to bring everyone back to task and let them know our exact position on the project.

INDUSTRY-WIDE COMMUNICATIONS EFFORTS

Today, the Internet has become the standard for presenting portfolios and for introducing the design firm and its various resources. It has become key to almost every part of our business. The Internet is constantly used by clients and others to reference our products or services.

Some designers present their very best work on the Internet. Others use it as an introduction and encourage prospective clients to contact the firm for additional information. Some very small design firms have such excellent Web sites that they appear large and extremely professional.

The American Society for Interior Designers (ASID) Web site now provides a designer referral service. ASID members can create a personal profile with project pictures and descriptions of their work, specialties, fee structure, education and experience, and business approach. Clients visiting the site can search for designers meeting their specific project criteria by filling out a short form.

The Interior Design Society (IDS) allows members to purchase a four page Web site designed specifically for their firms. For a set price, a firm can submit up to eight photos, logo artwork, and any further information it wants to appear on the site. A company contracted by IDS will design a Web site for the firm.

LISTENING

Relationships are based on communication. Listening to the people who are trying to communicate with us is what counts.

We all need to work at listening. Sometimes we're too busy or too excited about something to wait for a clear explanation. Sometimes we're simply torn between too many things to be good listeners.

Many extremely successful people who seem to have achieved most of what they want from life are great listeners. They're the people who make you feel as if you're the only person in the world who matters and the only one they care about during the time you're speaking with them.

This is a wonderful ability, especially for design professionals. We build relationships with our clients, gaining their trust and confidence. They have to feel that they are important to us.

Listening is so important a tool in building relationships that every design studio should have someone review its listening skills. Bring in a consultant, even if only on a monthly basis. Let this person talk with you and your staff, listen to your phone conversations, and see how well you communicate. The consultant could offer everyone suggestions for improving listening and other communication skills.

There are so many things we do every day without thinking because we're so involved in our work. We can develop bad habits that ruin aspects of our relationships without meaning or wanting to.

The following are some tips for good listening.

- Maintain eye contact with the person you're speaking with, and be aware of body language and expressions.
- Do you interrupt people? Do you start to speak before they have finished? The other person has a special thought to share with you. Are you letting him or her fully express that thought?
- Do you sometimes speak about things other people don't want to hear about? Designers can be so interested in a particular aspect of a project, they go on and on explaining all the details, while the client's interests lie in a completely different area. Consider what's important to a client before you explain details for hours.
- Avoid doing distracting things such as shuffling papers or moving things while other people are speaking. This is very annoying and can make the other person feel belittled.
- Dedicate your time and interest to the person on the other end of the phone. Try not to do three or four other things at the same time because you could miss important cues.
- Follow the conversation carefully, so you're not repeating something someone has previously said. You can, however, reiterate to enforce a point: You said that you were interested in . . . , therefore, how would this work?
- Keep your mind on the discussion. Sometimes you may be thinking about a color scheme, when all of a sudden the client is talking about another room or detail. We're creative people; this happens sometimes. When it does, admit it. Apologize for interrupting or being inattentive, then offer a possible solution if you have one. Making mistakes is human. Admitting them actually endears you to the other person.

We all need to improve our listening skills. We need mentors, consultants, guides—someone to direct us in improving how well we listen. No matter how old we are, we can always listen a bit better. High-tech communication tools are valuable in building quality relationships. But so is the ability to concentrate and listen to another person.

COMMUNICATION TOOLS

Technology makes communication fast and simple. All of this technology has changed response time from a matter of weeks to a matter of seconds. It's harder and harder to be out of touch.

Cellular Phones

Cell phones make communication very convenient. Being in constant contact with your office can save a lot of time and difficulty on projects. It permits us to be in touch wherever we are. But we must manage cell phones properly, or they can really be disruptive.

The prices of cellular phones have come down dramatically. Some of the early models cost approximately $3,000; now, in many cases, they're free or relatively inexpensive. Luxury cell phones are still expensive, but they permit us to take photos and videos, e-mail, play MP3 files, access the Web, and run programs. It's amazing what we can do with these new phones.

Voice Recorders

Tape recorders have come a long way since the days of bulky dictaphone machines. There are voice recorders the size of a credit card or pen. They're perfect when you want to leave a note or catch that creative thought before you forget it.

A good dictation style is something that needs to be learned. You want to record only what you'll need in your document. Make it easy for the person who transcribes the tape.

Many designers use pocket-sized recorders or their cell phones and PDAs to leave information for themselves or their staff. Digital voice recording can be done on an SD card.

Personal Digital Assistants and Handheld Computers

Pocket-sized personal computers vary widely in what they can do. Handheld PDAs send and receive messages, act as date-books, keep mailing lists, and run computer programs. Built-in WiFi allows users to access the Internet wirelessly, print documents, communicate with other Bluetooth devices, and create personal area networks using peer-to-peer communication. PDAs accept handwritten pen input as well as keyed input. Some even serve as a GPS system. Many people would be lost without them.

Portable Computers

Notebook computers let you work anywhere, anytime—except on airplanes during takeoffs and landings. Some pen-based portable computers have keyboards; some do not. Laptop computers fit easily onto your already crowded desk and can go with you to job sites as needed. They are also practical for voice dictation.

Designers now carry their laptops or PDAs to enable them to perform many services that would have required a well-equipped office in the past. This technology permits greater accuracy and easier changes. The role of the traditional secretary has been taken over by computers as software improves.

Peripherals

Anything that isn't already in your computer is a peripheral—your printer, fax, and mouse, for example.

Inkjet printers offer near-perfect quality printing, but it's water soluble. Laser printers are the Cadillac of printers. If you need to print building plans, special printers are called for.

The creation of the iPod has made the computer a standard for multimedia. Sophisticated speaker systems make game playing, music listening, and TV and movie watching theater-quality.

Scanners allow you to enter information and graphics into a computer without keyboarding. Optical character recognition (OCR) scanners recognize typefaces and type sizes. Without OCR, print is just a pattern of dots to the computer. OCR scanners allow you to record information in the format of your word processor. Scanners are available in flatbed and sheet-fed.

Electronic Resources

Future applications for the interior design field will include interacting with our vendors to send and receive up-to-date information, such as the latest research done in factories and testing centers. A service providing this could inform us about projects around the world and about the applications of certain types of products to specific situations. Information that once came to us via catalog a few times a year could be updated at a second's notice.

Any article, book, or government document published within the last four years can probably be retrieved through online databases. Libraries carry the more widely used databases. Examples include Dun and Bradstreet, offering financial information on businesses; ABI/Inform, an index and abstracts of 850 business and trade journals; and Infotrak, an index of popular publications such as the *Wall Street Journal*. Some databases are subscriber-based.

How Do You Find the Right Computer System?

Choosing the right computer system has become much simpler. You can now configure your computer online through manufacturer Web sites or through a local reseller. You can pick and choose the features you want to customize the computer for your needs.

The basic computer setup for either a PC or MAC operating system includes a computer with monitor, keyboard, and mouse; a printer; dual core processor; audio/video on motherboard; on board 10/100 LAN; on board wireless; DVD writer; CD-ROM reader; and 2–4 USB Ports. Get as much memory as you can afford, and try to buy an upgradeable system. Most designers need a word processing program, database manager, and graphics program. You'll have to decide whether to network with other designers in your firm or run independently.

Experts advise you to find your software first and then buy the computer you need to run it on. If the software calls for X amount of RAM (active memory, as opposed to storage memory), you'll need at least that much. Otherwise, the program will either run slowly or freeze up the computer.

Decide whether the standard monitor is large enough, or whether you'll need a larger one. The twenty-one-inch monitor is recommended for presentation work. The slim LCD monitors have now become standard.

Buying a computer and software is no longer labor-intensive. All the information you need is online. It's still a matter of researching what's available and then physically testing the computers to develop a preference.

You no longer have to be a computer programmer, engineer, or technophile to set up a computer. The computer industry standard is now what they call "plug and play." You take the boxes home, hook up the cables, and turn on the machine. Then you spend a couple of hours loading it with the appropriate software, although many computer manufacturers are now shipping computers with software preloaded.

If you're buying your first computer or are unhappy with your current system, talk with other design firms. See what they have, what they like, and why they like it. Go to computer stores, and look at computers. Personal preference is the best indicator. Test the keyboard. Do you have to pound the keys, or are they easy to use? Does the mouse fit your hand? Is it immediately responsive?

In some industries, professional organizations have polled their membership on the types of computers and programs they were using and published the results with recommendations and reasons. Some industries have developed proprietary software applications that demand a certain computer operating system. All of this helps narrow our selections.

You may want to speak with a local reseller or do research online. Some resellers will customize the applications as well as recommend computers, peripherals, and software. Some software firms include training with their software packages.

No matter what, learn to use your computer. It's a timesaver with a memory that can hold far more than yours.

CHAPTER 12

THE DESIGN TEAM

People and knowledge are a firm's greatest assets. You're often closer to the people you work with than to extended family, casual friends, or neighbors because you spend so much more time with them. Co-workers share some of our great passions. During personal tragedies, the people at work are often the ones who become part of your support system.

The group we work with becomes part of an extended family. This should be considered when selecting where we want to work, whom we employ, and which independent contractors will be part of the design team.

In the design company today, people are key—both staff and clients. Every member of our design team, from clients and staff to craftspeople and suppliers, must feel important to the project and be empowered and rewarded by the experience.

Every project is an opportunity to learn and develop our individual abilities. Knowledge is important, and we should always be ready to master a new process or procedure. Making mistakes is often a part of gaining mastery.

The design firm of today must be structured to produce the project. The process must be a coalition of the design team and the client. It's also important that each project is challenging to the various members of the design staff, so they're able to show their excellent talents as well as their excitement in developing it. This is the vision and the mission for today's design firm.

Technology has erased many of the boundaries of the past. We now have opportunities to interact, communicate, and perform more quickly and accurately than ever. Our work is much more complex than it used to be. We've had to become smarter and more independent. Because decisions are being made at all levels, everyone in the company must be well informed and qualified to make decisions. At one time, one person held most of the responsibility, so you had to return to the office for that project leader's decision. Today information is available to everyone on the team at the same time.

Today, there is also greater flexibility in our work styles, so they fit our personal preferences. This allows us flexible hours, multiple locations to work from, and compensation by the project. But no matter what else changes, we still have to get the job done. The key to business today is the ability to deal with things quickly using the talents, excitement, and energy of all of the people who work with us. It's not the time for large companies with heavy overheads. It *is* the time for groups with the ability to move quickly and intelligently.

DEFINING THE TEAM

Rather than thinking about their own preferences, the members of a design team need to understand they're working with the client—that the client is the key to the design process. This realization provides direction. The team solves the problem and answers the requests of the client. In addition, it is often the responsibility of the design team to go beyond what clients have asked for and show them other possibilities. We are clients' visionaries. We often must take them several steps beyond the problem they think they're solving and show them there are other creative and exciting systems that will work in their projects.

Design teams are led by a vision shared by all members. Some new systems of business management take on this model, which is based on the traditional approach of design teams: define the problem and build a team of the best people to solve it.

Someone has to take responsibility for a project; usually the team organizer serves as the leader or facilitator. The team itself may select a leader or allow leadership to pass to the person with the greatest expertise in that given area.

Teamwork isn't attending meetings and taking notes; it's working with a common purpose, a sense of interdependence, and shared accountability.

The interdisciplinary nature of design means you'll be building and rebuilding new teams for almost every project.

The core of your team, designers and support staff, may stay the same, whereas contractors, vendors, and clients may vary.

In building a team of people to work together on design projects, research and experience will show you how the pieces fit together. You can't arbitrarily throw people and vendors together and have it magically work. Sometimes it will, but just as often these unplanned partnerships fail because the prospective team members don't have the correct skills to make effective team members.

There is often resistance to the team concept from people who have been operating within a traditional organization. They may be concerned about managers' loss of control since very often a younger employee or junior specialist becomes a group leader, rather than the traditional manager who had always held the title. Compensation and reward are often based on team performance rather than long-term employment.

Complementary skills are important, and each team member should acquire the ability to look at things from more than one point of view. As the team evolves, it will develop its own standards of measurement and acceptable behavior. Success or failure becomes the joint responsibility of an intelligence-based staff.

Design Communities

The company may be called a "design community" because everyone who's there wants to work together. It's not necessarily a group without leaders. In fact, there is probably more than one person in charge. An ideal team is made up of people with different capabilities who work toward the same goal, contributing their talents when they're needed. This is an environment in which it's safe to demonstrate abilities and practice skills. Sometimes we make mistakes, but the design community and environment allow us to take chances, learn from our mistakes, and grow. This type of organization builds an experienced team.

Although design firms grow by expanding the disciplines they offer, you don't necessarily have to be the sole employer of everyone on your team. You may have to develop specialties in-house because they aren't available in your geographic area. On the other hand, having an in-house specialist may damage your relationships with other consultants. If you have an architect on staff, for example, many other architects may be hesitant to give you work because they see your practice as competing with theirs. If you're exclusively an interior design firm, these other specialists will see you as a partner, rather than a competitor.

Vendors and craftspeople are also members of the team, sharing the desire to complete projects efficiently and with high quality. We cannot afford to put our vendors and craftspeople in an antagonistic position. If we're going to achieve our goals in this competitive market, the vendors and craftspeople we work with have to be part of our company, bound by a marriage of respect and understanding.

In the past, adversarial relationships with vendors were accepted. The system encouraged it. Today, we cannot succeed without teamwork. We'll have fewer resources, but they will be much more important to us. Everything is based on relationships—relationships with substance.

A community or a company is a part of an evolving process, and not just a building or a location. Your company may have many types of organizational structures, but it must be made up of people who are involved and committed to the process of mastering a given subject for a particular goal. Success or failure in building a company team depends in part on the ability of the players to communicate. Change may cause confusion or chaos. This is often part of the trial-and-error process. The more we work together, the more we see the value of our team members' skills. The result is better projects.

LEADERSHIP

The goal of management is not to empower
subordinates but to
liberate them.

—DR. OREN HARARI

At first I didn't agree with Oren Harari, a professor at the Graduate School of Business in the University of San Francisco and a professional speaker. After I thought about it, I began to see that what he says is true, especially for the interior design discipline.

Designers want freedom. We want the excitement that comes from developing our talents, and we need the freedom to do it any way we want, not as someone else thinks it should be done. If we really want our teammates to use their talents, we have to give them opportunities to develop these talents. Of course we want a favorable outcome for our efforts, but developing leaders means allowing our team members to learn from their own mistakes.

To lead people, we have to listen to them and respect their opinions. Liberation grows out of self-confidence. Knowing our strengths and weaknesses allows us to relate better to the people on our teams. We really can't be good leaders without confidence in ourselves.

Arthur Ashe said that each time he went out to play tennis, he would try to do one or two things better than he had done them before. He never tried for a 100 percent improvement, but just to be a little better. A steady 3 percent improvement over time made Ashe a top tennis player. I think good leaders also try to top themselves every day.

Enthusiasm is important. I don't want to follow someone who's not enthusiastic or excited, nor someone who pounces on my mistakes in public and praises me in private. An energetic leader looks for the opportunity to compliment, develop, and encourage other people. An effective leader can sell anyone on an idea or a product.

Many successful people say they're careful not to expose themselves to negativity. I think this is extremely important. We need to surround ourselves with people who add to our abilities, whose attitudes nurture us. This is a hard thing to achieve, but it's worth working on.

You don't have to be an executive leader of a large corporation to be a leader in our industry. You can lead from many different positions. Some designers who run very small firms in small communities are doing exceptional work at leading and growing our industry in phenomenal ways. They find the right people and make sure they're doing a good job. These leaders build really strong teams, which can accomplish incredible things. It isn't a matter of title; it's a matter of knowing what it takes to do a job, putting the right team together, and leading the team in a professional way.

If there are unproductive people in your group, get them out. Team members who are mediocre or problematic can only destroy the rest of the structure.

Howard Gardner, a famous educator and author of *Five Minds for the Future*,[1] stated that if people invested more time in being interested, rather than interesting, they would be much more successful. This is so true in the interior design field. Designers who become involved in their clients' lives and are part of their growth are more likely to work on more numerous, bigger, and more exciting projects in the future. These designers will never want for work.

I-Power

I-Power is a management concept that involves asking everyone in the company to come up with ideas to improve it. The focus is on gathering small ideas and giving an immediate response. The goal is a free and easy exchange of views. The company benefits in two ways: (1) through the shared ideas and (2) through the team spirit this approach fosters.

The I-Power program puts the power to change in the hands of people with practical experience. In the beginning, workers are often skeptical, thinking this is just another words-rather-than-action program. But there are small rewards distributed monthly for ideas that are accepted and used. The monthly awards publicize the program, ideas, and accomplishments. I-Power gets people involved in a team process by testing ideas as a standard practice. People like putting their own ideas into action, more so than having them taken over by a hierarchical system.

In larger companies, each person is given I-power pads. I-Power suggestion boxes are placed where they cannot be missed. To get the ball rolling, the leader may suggest areas that need improvement. Employees have access to a selection of publications and videos to use as reference materials, so when they know something is wrong but don't have an answer to fix it, they aren't limited by their own experience.

Elements of the I-Power program will adapt easily into the work styles of most interior designers because it is very much like the studio system of learning. It's normal for us to discuss a problem with everyone in the firm and then ask for ideas. The people who are most familiar with a particular process often have ideas on how to streamline it. This system promotes individual responsibility. If I'm away from my desk and a member of my staff knows the answer to a client's question, the client does not have to wait until I return.

The I-Power program was developed by Martin Edelston, president of Boardroom Inc., and continues to be a very effective system of improving the way people work together. Edelston uses I-Power in his own company with great success. He has written a book and developed courses in which the system is taught.

Taking the Lead

> *Leadership is much more an art, a belief, a condition of the heart, than a set of things to do. The visible signs of artful leadership are represented ulti-mately in its practice.*
>
> —MAX DEPREE

Not everyone in a group will be interested in, or capable of, creating new opportunities for business; someone must take the lead. Most people prefer a stable working environment; changes make them uncomfortable. Also, most people don't have the interpersonal skills to be leaders.

It usually takes a strong person to lead a group in the formation of a communal design firm. After the firm is created, its leaders share the burdens and rewards of responsibility. In the end, the initiator works much more as facilitator or coach than as a "dictator."

People want four things from their leaders: direction, meaning, hope, and results, according to Peter F. Drucker, in his book *Managing a Non-Profit Organization.*[2]

An organization based on teamwork must have a philosophy—a set of values with which it operates. Developing a direction and inspiring others to work with you in achieving that set of values is important to your organization. This must happen at every level. It's the responsibility of each of us to develop this philosophy.

Four main elements are part of a successfully decentralized company:

- Shared responsibility within an organization works best when the objective is on target. The objective should meet the individual needs, values, and goals of the various members of the group. Each of us must see and believe that our work is worth doing, creating, and devoting our lives to.
- Each of us must be committed to the same goal. It has to be easy, simple, and clear.
- We must communicate the goal. We must be able to get other people to invest in this shared vision.
- We must encourage and reinforce our efforts because progress is never a straight line. Progress needs constant reminders and reinforcements.

As designers, we have all worked on projects in which the client says, "I did it myself." We have to learn to take this as a compliment. Lao-tzu, in the *Tao Te Ching*, wrote, "True leaders inspire others to do great things and, when the work is done, their people proudly say, 'we did this ourselves.'" Designers are called into leadership roles in many different ways. But we direct, encourage, and lead people to perform and do things far beyond what they would or could have done without us. We create the shared vision and often assist with the process, to the point that "designer" is synonymous with "leader."

We also have to follow at times, take the directions our clients give us, and understand the opportunities and limitations of our craft and of nature. It is our job all the while, however, to be leaders. I think we have now learned to follow only someone whose values and philosophies are similar to our own. Follow someone you can respect.

Managers are people who do things the right way. Leaders are people who do the right things. Peter Drucker said that leadership is a matter of how to be and not how to do. He says leadership is ethics in practice full time.

A great leader doesn't waste the time of other people, whether they're staff or clients. The vision must be projected clearly enough to direct people effectively. Leaders must take the time to clarify what they want done. Define your own personal objectives and mission first. You can't possibly share something you haven't thought through clearly.

It's a step in the right direction to define problems. In so doing, you'll have an easier time finding the key to what your firm can do to handle these problems successfully.

When you don't get an appropriate response to a request, find another way to phrase it or to get something done. There's no point in blaming other people. Either you did not present your request properly or the structure doesn't exist for you to receive the appropriate response.

Getting the best from people means defining the specific results you want. Everyone must share your concept of success. It isn't enough to say, Do the best you can. That's abstract and too hard to interpret.

Reinforce good performance by letting people know you really appreciate their efforts. Positive reinforcement is worth more than any other kind of interaction.

Shall I Lead?

A leader doesn't have to be the chief executive officer of the company, but each group needs someone with the power and ability to make things happen. A leader can develop from almost any part of the company.

The team approach to doing business and the leader-follower approach are similar. Max DePree wrote in his book *Leadership Is an Art,*[3] "The first responsibility of a leader is to define reality. The last is to say thank you. In between, the leader must become a servant and a debtor. That sums up the progress of an artful leader."

The leader's job is to keep everyone's attention on the process. Leaders must be visionaries; they set goals; they're in front moving, sharing, dreaming, and creating the mission.

Rainmakers

The interior design and furnishings field has not trained, developed, or created many rainmakers. Yet, the success of a firm strongly depends on them. We need people who actually create a need—not just sell or respond to it. We have people who know how to make a project happen but few who know how to drum up a need for our services. The client must be convinced that your firm is the best for the job.

CONSULTANTS ON CALL

In this fast-moving, action-oriented, information-based era, teams form and re-form constantly. We are blending the cultures of our clients, the design world (not just interior design, but all other design disciplines), crafts, and our resources.

For a team to work efficiently, there must be rapport and mutual respect among its members. In the extended team of designers, craftspeople, and vendors, everyone stands up for his or her own industry and is right to do so. Someone must make a judgment call. On every project there are limits. We have only so much money. We have only so much space. We have only so much whatever. So who determines the best "buy" for the client in a given situation?

Often the interior designer is the person making the decisions with the help of respected consultants he or she knows and trusts. We don't want to make decisions based on information from somebody who is new to the group. We want to see other projects by this potential teammate. We want to know who has worked with the person we're considering. We want indicators that allow us to judge how much we can rely on this person's information.

Your search may begin with a directory of consultants. Next, check their references, including a list of projects they've worked on and with which firms. Unfortunately, this research takes time, and it does get expensive. When I take a project, I try to anticipate the weak areas and the specific demands of the project with which we may not have experience. I use Pareto's 80/20 ratio—only 20 percent of the project should be a totally new experience for us.

The same ratio applies to consultants. Eighty percent of your consultants should be people and firms you have worked with before; you know them and the issues you can trust their judgment on.

The new person brought into the team is your 20 percent; the rest of the team is your 80 percent.

Groups That Can Refer You to Accredited Consultants

Institute of Management Consultants USA
2025 M Street, NW, Suite 800
Washington, DC 20036-3309
(202) 367-1134 or (800) 221-2557
www.imcusa.org

American Consultants League
c/o ETR
245 NE 4th Avenue
Suite 102
Delray Beach, FL 33483
http://americanconsultantsleague.com

The Consultants Bureau
P.O. Box 10057
New Brunswick, New Jersey 08906-0057
www.consultantsbureau.org

WHAT MAKES A GOOD TEAM MEMBER?

If you like a person, chances are your client will like that person too. If something about that person makes you uncomfortable, your client will probably feel the same way. In building your team, think about what makes a good team member.

How well do prospective team members express themselves? The people who work with you should have good communication skills. Do they appear enthusiastic and encouraging? Do they relate to you in the way you'd like to see them relate to clients? Are they able to explain design in terms clients will understand? Look at these variables as well as at their work and educational experiences before you consider adding designers or contractors to your team.

It's been said that the collective IQ of a team is half that of the least intelligent team member. It's something to consider when forming your team.

Sometimes a great candidate shows up at the wrong time or isn't right for the project. Job applicants whose skills and knowledge challenge your team may seem great on their own, but sometimes they simply don't fit in. I think we do need to be challenged, but let's be careful whom we select to challenge us.

Some people say they can do something when they actually have no experience with it. As the head of a firm or team leader, we're responsible for reviewing these individuals' abilities and determining just what they can really do. Résumés and portfolios can be deceptive. While you may be familiar with the name of the design school or the project, how do you know the precise curriculum or the scope of the applicant's responsibilities?

Rather than be surprised during the project, speak with the prospective team member's former employers before making any hiring decision. This does require written permission. To protect your company, you must have appropriate permission forms signed. Some sample forms are in my book *The Interior Design Business Handbook,* fourth edition. Ask applicants for the names of the people at their previous jobs who knew them best and if it's all right to contact them. Determine if prospective team members' present employers know the applicants are looking for another position.

For both prospective employees and contractors, obtain as much information as you can. Visit a project the applicant is involved in; don't just look at a photograph. The site will give you many clues. Find out what kind of clients the applicant has been working with. Find a way to speak with some of these clients, and learn what the clients think of the applicant.

Tom Peters advises that the next time a job candidate with a great resume and the potential for creativity dozes off during an interview, wake him up and hire him. It was you who put him to sleep.[4] The point is that we need people who are excited by life, who design for the new world. We need people who use their imaginations to develop that world, rather than simply trying to please the market.

Every Team Member Must Be a Business Person

It's best if every team member understands business issues. It makes it much easier for everyone to work together if people realize the costs involved in getting things done. Team members need to know precisely the services you offer and exactly what it means to run the firm in a profitable manner. By "profitable" I mean not just financially, but exposure to different kinds of work, and staff-development opportunities.

Internships

Under the Fair Labor Standard, any firm that uses student interns must meet certain conditions. A student cannot replace a regular employee and is not guaranteed a job at the end of his or her internship. Both the company and the intern must be aware that the intern isn't entitled to income during the internship. However, you may choose to pay interns a lump sum to be applied toward their future education. The intern must receive some training from your company, and this training should be comparable to what he or she would receive at a design school. Most importantly, the training of interns is the primary goal—not necessarily having them work for your company. The student intern must learn procedural skills.

Independent Contractors

Today so many professionals, especially accomplished ones, prefer to work as independent contractors. Not directly employed, they join your team and fill a specific need on a specific project. When that project is finished, they want to go on and work with other firms. This permits them to work the way that's most productive for their particular disciplines and offers them the flexibility many creative people want. Professionals who were once associated with small firms have, either through demand or choice, selected this style of working. As we move forward, we will see more and more independent contractors who do what it takes to get the job done and then get paid for the job. We interior designers have been doing this throughout our careers. We don't really have the security in our jobs that other professionals may have. We don't have tenure, a guaranteed salary, or a retirement plan. We're used to completing a project and moving on.

If you're an independent designer who leads a design firm, it's essential to have independent contractor forms signed by anyone working with your firm. These forms define the work to be done, who's responsible for what, and the method of compensation.

This brings up the question of employment structures and taxes. Independent contractors normally carry their own insurance and pay their own taxes. The Internal Revenue

Service often questions firms run on this basis, because the IRS much prefers to see many of these contractors listed as employees. It's important to have up-to-date documentation. The IRS believes that a person who earns his or her entire income for the year from your firm is an employee. Unless it's clear that the person works for other firms and not just yours, there could be problems.

HANDLING ORGANIZATIONAL CONFLICTS

When groups move or change in any way, some of the organizational structure is automatically destroyed. In many cases, the structure has taken years to build. How do you ease the transition? If you simply add another person, you create feelings of job insecurity among the existing staff. They may resist necessary changes. But if you set a time limit on the relationship and make it clear that the new person is there only to help manage the transition, you make it easier for the staff to accept his or her suggestions. Easier, in fact, than if you, the CEO, made the suggestions.

A nearby firm recently combined two offices that were only five miles apart. There was no reason their clients could not drive that extra five miles. Combining the facilities freed money to use on additional equipment. Integrating the staff simplified communications. Logistically and financially, joining the two offices made sense.

But the offices had been run as two completely separate structures. Anticipating clashes in management styles, one of the senior partners decided the firm needed a professional manager. The existing management had run the organization for years reasonably well. They had personal relationships with the senior partners. When a new management person was brought in at a level above the existing managers, they were cut out of the loop and resented it. Bringing in another boss who is being paid two or three times what the rest of the staff makes may only cause a firm to fall apart. I've seen this happen many times.

Combining staffs is very difficult if done without preparation. The circumstances described above probably would have worked better had the firm in question brought in a consultant—an interim person rather than a permanent new boss—to help it reorganize, adjust, and improve efficiency. Some firms even bring in transition teams for a limited time. If there's an understanding that the team members are there as trainers only, you can avoid unrest and fear among your managers that their positions are in jeopardy.

For example, to resolve a conflict, some parishes won't permit a church to take on a new pastor. They hire an interim pastor to work with the church for one or two years and work out the problems. Then they bring in a permanent person.

Change increases the pressures on everyone in the office. CEOs and senior staff worry where the income is coming from and are very aware of how much work they must produce to generate that income. They juggle legal issues, government labor regulations, and myriad other everyday pressures. Employees fear for their jobs. Everyone is under pressure. We need to protect both the staff and professionals by removing some of these pressures and restoring the pleasures of working—otherwise, the designs and the firm will suffer.

With any change in a management system, there are, inevitably, some people who will no longer fit in as well as they used to. Even if you have precisely the right staff for team management, the transition can be rough. It's a major adjustment, both for the staff and for the leader. In this situation, a consultant-trainer could help employees see new opportunities to contribute.

Business therapists specialize in management problems. They're often psychotherapists with a business background who move into a company and work to solve its problems. Outside people are usually more effective. They can be more objective and take positions that a person who's a regular part of the team can't take as easily. These therapists look at change and conflict as problems with resolutions. They scrutinize organizations and suggest ways to accustom existing staff to new work styles and new demands.

In the top-down style of management, you could say, This person is out, and that person is in. But unless an employee is actively destructive, why would you do that? If the person has been working with you for ten years or longer, he or she has valuable knowledge about the way your firm works. The employee could help ease the transition once he or she is reoriented.

Branches of the Design Industry

All branches of the design industry, including interior design, architecture, and their various subspecialties, should form closer bonds with one another so that:

- We understand each other's practices.
- We can use each other's products better.
- We can produce a higher quality of work.
- We can make better use of time, energy, and money.
- We can stimulate each other.
- We can close the information gap between manufacturers and consumers, so manufacturers produce what consumers want.
- We can all learn from each other.
- We can prevent mistakes.
- We can surpass what we're capable of individually.
- We can create products of higher value.
- We can bring the benefits of design to all people.

Notes

1. Howard Gardner. *Five Minds for the Future.* Boston: Harvard Business School Press, 2006.
2. Peter F. Drucker. *Managing a Non-Profit Organization.* New York: HarperCollins, 1990.
3. Max DePree. *Leadership Is an Art.* New York: Doubleday, 1989.
4. Tom Peters. "Peters on Excellence," *Central Penn Business Journal,* April 18, 1994, p. 45.

CHAPTER 13

DIRECTIONS

The way we work has changed considerably. Many of us have changed our systems because of our specialties or because of the availability of information through technology. The kinds of clients and projects we receive have also forced tremendous changes. It's worthwhile to compare different ways of working that may be appropriate to our practices. We need to also consider our relationship with industry.

PARTNERS IN INDUSTRY

Today, most firms are doing more work with fewer staff members, often with less time and money. This isn't unique to the design field; it's definitive of business today. In order to manage heavier responsibilities, design firms need stronger ties to their resources.

A team made up of marketing people, engineers, office staff, and installers can strengthen the interior design firm. People on the same team share information; collaboration speeds the process. As we have discussed extensively in the last chapter about design teams, and throughout the book, the individuals on your team—whether they work for your firm, consult with you, or provide you with needed materials—will bring their expertise to your project, allowing you to find out about new products and processes, and to provide your client with needed information.

You can only design with what you know. If you don't know the features of materials and products, you can't properly incorporate them into your design. Our projects demand specific information. Exploring and investigating new products and materials are basic parts of design.

There's a tremendous amount of research involved in any project. There's a demand for much more detailed specifications and reasons to select a particular product.

Our resources can be part of our research committees, alerting us to newly available products and to vendors we may not have previously worked with. The experience vendors have with products can help determine the feasibility of a given project, in terms of cost and performance.

Our resources can supply all types of code information and create a context that helps us judge when their products fit our projects. They also have detailed specifications on file. These can be faxed or sent to us by e-mail, which saves time. Their experience on a range of projects may lead them to suggest possible product modifications or other products in their lines.

Resources can easily furnish the information through samples, technical data, specifications, and details. They probably know from experience how their products can be combined with other products. They know their competition; they probably also know of product lines that work well with theirs.

Our resources can provide budget information as we develop a project, so that we can determine the budget before the design is complete. Most resources have all this information on their Web sites. Designers can access it at any time. Product specifications and details also can be accessed and downloaded.

Difference in Cost and Quality

We need to understand in detail why one piece of furniture costs $12,000, whereas a similar piece costs only $2,000. We need to be able to give our client well-informed reasons for the differences in cost and quality of the pieces we present.

Manufacturers sponsor tours and trips so designers can learn the production story in detail. We need to make time for such trips in our research schedules.

In exchange, designers should make every effort to inform resources of the exact demands being placed on their products in a specific installation. We should tell manufacturers' representatives how their products work in our projects, especially when they work well. When a minor modification updates a product or makes it more usable, pass that information along.

Anytime a client brings a problem to your attention, ask for specifics. Check with your resource. Are you the only one who has run into this problem, or have other designers as well? Is this a recent development, or has it been going on for a while? What does the resource think you should do about the problem?

We should happily do anything we can to improve the flow of information in our industry to ensure that we are using the best products.

FUTURE WORK STYLES

For each project we do, we often form new teams of carpenters, cabinetmakers, plumbers, electricians, marble workers, and other craftspeople. A system for rating qualifications and skills can make hiring unknown craftspeople less of a gamble. It can work not only for the craftspeople, but for entire companies. When hiring a company, individual skill ratings allow us to know how qualified the workers are to deal with our type of project. This information needs to be available on both union and nonunion workers.

Skill Ratings

We'd like to see more systems like the traditional guild of medieval Europe, which included apprentices, journeymen, and master craftsmen. In a guild system, members are defined by their skill levels. When you hired a Level 1 or a Level 6 person, you knew what level of work they were capable of producing. This was both good for those doing the hiring and the crafts. Craftsmen could move around the country, from project to project, without losing their positioning.

In the past, the guild or union was responsible for devising the requirements for a training program as well as for grading and rating systems. Craftsmen were ranked according to recommendations of master craftsmen and their actual work experience.

When you do a wide variety of projects, the guild system is needed. If you're a specialist and offer turnkey service, your craftspeople may work only for your company.

What if there was an internal rating system of skills levels for designers and allied craftspeople? A designer who excels at specifying fabrics and furniture placement has skills that are different from one who develops interior space requirements for a specific use.

Designers now have qualifying exams, such as the NCIDQ (National Council for Interior Design Qualification) or other state-controlled testing. Some specialists, such as kitchen designers, have a specific qualifying exam as well. More specialists need to undergo qualifying testing and meet standards that are easily understood by the public. In many cases, there's no objective way for us to know, and no way for the public to know, what skill level we've achieved. There's no way for designers to know at a glance who to add to our teams for specific projects.

There's a need to distinguish between decorators, whose real skill is an inventive use of color and fabric, and designers who are capable of planning the requirements and specifications of corporate campuses for the largest Fortune 500 firms. There's a need, too, for all the levels in between.

Larger design firms use an informal rating system for project designers and design assistants. A more formal skills rating system can only help the industry. Because the staffs of companies are so fluid, we need to know that Designer A can handle construction management. We need to know that Designer B is excellent in the planning stages for giant projects but also that he or she is fully qualified to handle residential and commercial design projects up to a certain level of complexity.

Giving the public a single meaning for the word "designer" creates an identity. But within that umbrella term there are many types of designers. We don't all have the same aptitudes or training. There are designers who are better at finish work or dressing a room than at construction detailing. Rather than insist that all of us perform at exactly the same level, let's be realistic and recognize our differences.

Showroom of Today

Charlotte Moss, a noted New York City interior designer, is leading a trend. She has opened a shop that's really a townhouse—a five-story townhouse on Manhattan's Upper West Side set up like a house. Almost everything in every room is for sale. Many of the objects are her own products— running from the very inexpensive to one-of-a-kind pieces that cost more than $50,000. Moss features gift and garden items, as well as clothing. But principally she offers interior items, ranging from linens to china to bedroom objects. Many were collected during her world travels. We will be seeing more of this type of showroom throughout the country, focusing on the individual styles of designers.

Interior Designers Could Use Agents

The acting profession has agents; why not interior design? The system in which the agents know the strengths of a designer and find him or her appropriate work would be excellent for our field. Karen Fisher's Designer Previews, Charlotte Peters Inc., and Designer Referral of New York are designer referral agencies. They present designers' portfolios to potential clients, finding and making matches.

Just as designers have had to expand and change their services, referral agencies may grow and change into full-service agents. Some may offer career advice. They might suggest that designers pursue specific types of projects, get additional training, or pair up with other specialists. For example, an agent may tell a designer, This is your strong spot; this is the way I see your business going, and these are the places I see you fitting in best. Therefore, let's go after these types of jobs.

Agents could have the skills to look at your educational background and experience and get to know you as a person. They then can guide you as a mentor, coach, or career developer. Agency work may not be done by a single person, but by a group. One person might provide the educational direction; a second might make matches with other specialists. Yet a third might offer advice on sales and marketing presentations.

Interior designers love to design. Most of us don't want to interrupt our directed creative efforts to search for the right client. Once potential clients have been screened, we're willing to learn the material, rehearse, make a great presentation, and really study the job. But some of that screening could be done better by agents.

A few years ago employment agencies and headhunters, such as The Viscusi Group, dealt in career positions. Now they also make temporary placements for the term of projects. There's been a change in the way designers are employed and the way design employment agencies operate. Full-service design employment/placement agencies that offer advice about career strategy, market placement, and recommend profitable teams would have a niche.

An outside consultant specializing in designer firms can help evaluate your goals, objectives, and abilities to help guide you toward appropriate opportunities. This consultant could also help you with organizational processes, such as time management and programming the different tasks required to complete a project. The consultant might also recommend professional groups, such as our Designer's Business Forum, to provide support materials and opportunities.

Group Practices

The demands on our field today are so great, we have to use every tool available. Technology is essential in many design processes, but it can never replace personal relationships. We need the spirited contact and the stimulation of people who share our goals or at least have complementary goals. That's one reason we visit furniture markets and design shows. But what do we have on a day-to-day basis?

Interior designers have always worked as independents, but this means we miss out on some opportunities. We're often deprived of contact with colleagues. That type of interaction is so important in nurturing the creative spirit. It's missing when a designer sits in his or her own house or studio, with no one else around. Designers who work in large firms have social interaction, but the vast majority of us don't.

We really need to associate with each other in some way, perhaps in a joint studio where designers could share materials and ideas. It's great to be at your own office and be able to stick to a project until it's finished. But there are other times when being among people is more important. Working alone isolates us from the ideas and intellectual stimulation needed to keep our skills up to date.

We all could gain from a human resource professional. This person could be a designer who has had experiences in creating opportunities for other designers and knows how to develop their abilities.

Internet, TV Programs, and Working Globally

Professional magazines are always reminding us that today's market is global. Our resources are global. We can specify products from anywhere in the world just as easily as we can items from local craftspeople.

But let's be practical. You can't leap into a global market without some preparation and a long-term commitment. It's true many designers have worked in other countries, and some practices have become global in the past few years. It's possible to duplicate a process you've done in the United States in another country, provided there's a team there you can work with.

It's also possible to work with people outside the United States if you understand each other's cultures. But if you don't understand the language and the social mores of the country, you'll be working with a handicap. Product designers and other designers working in other countries have been enrolling in language schools in increasing numbers.

Many design firms have offices in other countries, staffed with a talent pool of multicultural designers. These companies have spent years developing these relationships to meet the needs of different environments.

Consider the very deep cultural and philosophical aspects of design work. Consider the communications problems that can arise even when both you and your client speak American English. Proxemics—the study of social and personal space and man's perception of it—is a key part of interior design. Edward Hall, the anthropologist who coined the term, says, "People from different cultures not only speak different languages, but inhabit different sensory worlds." It's hard for any participatory process to develop without the common ground of a shared language.

Even when you speak the same language, cultural differences can stop you cold. There's a legendary story about American and British delegates arguing over whether to "table" a proposal. For the Americans, a "tabled" proposal was dead and done with. For the British, it was one put on the table for discussion.

There's a great difference in "global" attitudes between the United States and Japan. When a U.S. company goes into a foreign country, it sets up a factory that can run totally independently of the North American one. It may be run by native, non-North American officers. The company has been designed to fit into that country's culture. With Japanese organizations, even if the factory is here in the United States, it's still controlled by Japan. The company culture is Japanese, and so is the hierarchy.

There was a time when the link between companies was political; now it's economic. A lot of designer resources have strong relationships with other countries because of deep commitment to investments in those countries.

Most successful firms have some long-term relationships, including some very well-established clients both here and abroad. There may be resources you've worked with for years in a particular country. Or perhaps you've always been fascinated with its culture and visit the country every time you get a chance. You may have developed great friends there who are now your working partners.

In other words, there is a real commitment to working in that country. I'm not saying it's impossible to work in other countries. But it's usually costly and can even be counterproductive, unless you make a long-term investment and become part of their cultures.

Working abroad successfully takes a combination of the right people, knowledge of that particular country and outside resources who will assist in the process. You need three different kinds of people. First there are the explorers, the instigators—people who like to scout a new area and break the ice. Then there are the doers who turn the instigators' dreams into reality. Finally, there are residents of the country who deal with the day-to-day details of running a company and maintain relationships. That takes people with deep pockets.

Building the understanding, trust, and working relationships needed for interior design in general doesn't happen overnight. Establishing a base in another country often takes years.

CHAPTER 14

SPECIALIZATION AND SPECIALTIES IN INTERIOR DESIGN

At one time there were basically two specialties in interior design—residential and contract. Today there are many. Successful designers are usually specialized in a very small area. But with the help of technology, they are able to work easily throughout the world—assisting other designers, architects, and professionals.

The field of interior design has become very complex. Our field has reached the point that we have complete organizations dedicated to individual specialties. One great one is NKBA, the National Kitchen and Bath Association. The association presently has graduate and specialized courses for designing kitchens that require one to two years of total dedication just to that specialty. We're seeing many more such programs, as each one of the specialties becomes more sophisticated. I look forward to the day our professional associations encourage NCIDQ to test us on each of their specialties.

The following are the specialties with which I'm familiar. You may know of others. We'll continue to develop new specialties as our social and business structures demand them. It's stimulating and exciting to be in a field with such depth. We're different from our clients or the typical consumer who considers him or herself an interior designer. Our market today demands high-level work, and specializing permits us to give clients the quality work they desire and demand.

Many designers will combine two or three specialties but usually have one as their lead. Then, as the market interest in the lead area diminishes or fades, they can shift their primary focus to another one of their specialties. It's fascinating to see how our background directs us to a specialty and positions us to meet many special needs.

This is definitely a time for specialization. Designers with the greatest name recognition and financial success are those who have specialized. (This could lead you to wonder if being multifaceted in accomplishments and abilities hurts more than it helps.)

A review of design publications of the past ten years shows that less qualified design firms can and did take the market share from "better" firms just because they were very clear in stating that they just do offices, nothing but medical facilities, or only restaurants.

Specialization most often leads to better profit. Specialists know their work; it's easy because they have done it many times. The basics stay the same. You can vary certain facets of the design, but you don't have to relearn 80 percent of the process. This lowers the risk of error and speeds up design production.

The following pages offer brief looks at more than 100 areas of specialization.

ACOUSTIC DESIGN

Hearing is one of the five senses; sound is an integral part of every environment. As space becomes more expensive and people live and work closer together, quiet has become a luxury. Specialists in acoustic design consult on projects ranging from concert halls, conference rooms, open offices, and restaurants, to residential design. Controlling sound has become a science. In open-landscape offices, there are sound-breaking panels and sound maskers. Teleconferencing rooms need to contain sound. On the other hand, restaurants need a certain amount of noise to sell food. In any space, from residential to the most technologically demanding commercial environments, there are sounds we want to hear and sounds we don't want to hear.

ADAPTIVE REUSE

Reusing old buildings for new purposes is a growing trend as the composition of cities changes and there is greater concern for ecology and the preservation of available resources. Factory lofts are converted into shopping malls and residential use. It's not always practical to maintain an older commercial structure as commercial real estate. For example, turning the Chrysler Building into a residential condominium building is being seriously considered. The building's construction will not accommodate the way computers are used today in business. Workstations can only be functional within so many feet of the main terminal. This makes many major landmark buildings obsolete as office space, while their location and quality of construction argue that the buildings be reused.

ADMINISTRATIVE HEADQUARTERS

Every major company or organization has an administration building with needs and demands that require design. The needs and demands change as the products change, and interior designers are called in to streamline and develop spaces to support work flow. At one time, we just designed offices, but today social environments are also important. Sometimes, important decisions are made over a cup of coffee rather than in the boardroom.

AIRPLANE DESIGN

This is a unique specialty. Airplanes range from standard passenger carriers to flying conference rooms or living spaces. Designers must consider weight and fire safety, as well as psychological and environmental effects of design.

AMUSEMENT PARK DESIGN

Designers work on theme parks, developing the visual components that enhance rides and exhibits. These can incorporate animated figures and appeal to all the senses, even smell. These designers may develop unique signage for the park, design the fixtures, or be involved in service areas: food service, restrooms, and souvenir shops. Park design has this in common with museums and community buildings. Safety, effectiveness, and efficiency are important. Profitability is determined by the effectiveness of the fantasy, and everything has to work so that the fantasy is maintained. Designing traffic patterns to keep people moving is an art in itself.

With the high level of technology we have today, the amusement park experience has gone beyond anything we could have imagined. These designers are not just artistic; they are also very skilled in scientific thinking and computer knowledge and capabilities.

APARTMENT, CONDOMINIUM, AND CO-OP DESIGN

With more multiple-housing developments in every part of the country, this specialty presents major opportunities. Some interior designers do only apartment layouts; others do only lobbies and corridors. Still others are responsible for the communal areas, which include function rooms, social areas, televideo conference centers, computer rooms, office and secretarial areas, and athletic areas.

AQUARIUM DESIGN

This specialty is not limited to aquatic parks. There are designers who do large aquarium designs for homes, offices, and other businesses. There is a restaurant I know of in which one enters by walking over a sizable aquarium. Aquariums as a design element serve several purposes. Medical evidence suggests that gazing at an aquarium reduces blood pressure, and there also is a social push toward using natural, earth-friendly materials in public spaces.

ART CONSULTANT

Searching out existing art and contracting for the creation of new art suitable to a specific interior environment is the function of art consultants, who usually work for the client. They provide the background to support art investments. These specialists must have an extensive knowledge of fine art disciplines, as well as a practical and artistic understanding of interior design.

ART DEALING

Interior designers with an interest in fine art understand what people enjoy and will buy; they understand space and know how to place art properly. This is a major asset for an art dealer, because art sells best when it can be envisioned and placed in an interior.

AUDIOVISUAL CENTER DESIGN

Televisions, computers, videocassette recorders, and stereo equipment provide entertainment and worldwide communication for residential and commercial use. They are often clustered in the same area or room. The technical requirements of these devices demand a knowledge of electronics, acoustics, and lighting disciplines.

AUDITORIUM DESIGN

This is a fascinating field, and very different from stage design. Acoustics and sight lines in theater design are vital and complex. Productions can be made or destroyed by very small design elements of a house. With today's multimedia opportunities, this field has become very complex.

BARRIER-FREE DESIGN

Laws require that new commercial and public buildings, as well as renovations to existing buildings, make the space accessible to those in wheelchairs. Barrier-free design is increasingly desirable for all spaces. Probably more money has been invested in designing for the physically limited or orthopedically disabled than for any other group. Interior designers specialize in reviewing products and buildings to ensure that standards are met. This specialty is included in almost every project.

BATHROOM DESIGN

Once a neglected and utilitarian room, today the bathroom joins the kitchen as a selling point for houses. Modern bathrooms may include spa-like environments with whirlpool baths, saunas, and hot tubs. Public restrooms and bathrooms for commercial spaces demand state-of-the-art detailing. A new consciousness about human needs has greatly improved asepticism, safety, and the adaptations needed to make the bathroom barrier-free. International bathing customs have had an influence, bringing us European fixtures, the Oriental soaking tub, saunas, and steam rooms. Environmental concerns have brought about new products and codes.

BEAUTY SALON AND BARBERSHOP DESIGN

Beauty salons and barbershops are often mixed-media salons. The designer may be asked to provide appropriate space for services such as waxing, massage, facials, manicures, and cosmetology, in addition to hair care. State regulations and requirements differ. Interior designers in the beauty field often work with or for suppliers, who may offer complete financing and turnkey projects.

CAD SPECIALIST

A designer who is expert at computer-assisted design and drafting is increasingly valuable today. Computers are instrumental in communicating with other design professionals. Designs created on CAD may be used by the client as a basis for in-house space management. CAD's accuracy and ability to make quick changes is invaluable. Although there are still specialists, CAD has now become a basic tool of most designers.

CARPET AND RUG DESIGN

Who should know better how to design carpets and rugs than interior designers, who are responsible for a large volume of floor-covering projects? Interior designers working with textile specialists can develop the most suitable rugs for a given situation. Designing hand-woven rugs is very different from designing for the technical demands of Axminster, Wilton, tufted, woven, or printed machines. A designer must either study at a textile-intensive school, such as the Philadelphia Textile School, or work extensively in the carpet field.

CATALOG PRODUCT DESIGN

There are designers who design special products specifically for catalogs. Catalogs are now a major resource for consumers, whether they're in large cities or small provinces. Every consumer has piles of catalogs.

CERAMIC TILE DESIGN

This field encompasses foreign and domestic sources as well as artistically made and mass-produced tiles. Ceramic tiles are used for high-traffic, functional areas as well as for decorative effect, including murals and sculptures.

CLOSET DESIGN

Space is at a premium today, especially closet space. Around the country, businesses that do only closets are designing storage components and new ways to store almost every item.

CODE SAFETY DESIGN LAW

These specialists keep up-to-date information on building, fire, and safety codes in every state. They are familiar with the laws affecting these codes and may provide consultation to other designers, contractors, manufacturers, and owners.

COLOR CONSULTATION

Color and its effects on people are a recognized science with well-documented results. Color is the most noticed of all the design elements. This specialty is used by all design disciplines, as well as marketing firms, corporations, governments, and medical practices—anywhere the encouragement of specific psychological reactions is desired.

COMMERCIAL DESIGN

This specialty covers everything except residences—including retail, businesses, offices, laboratories, factories, medical facilities, and other commercial spaces. Most commercial designers specialize further. Within the specialty of medical design, for example, there are several subspecialties.

COMPUTER OFFICE DESIGN

Designing to accommodate computer use is much in demand. Office requirements of computers have changed dramatically since they first emerged in the workplace. In some ways, the requirements are less rigorous. Specialists who design offices to accommodate computers usually work for computer companies. These specialists may travel across the country to explain the requirements and conveniences of combining computer and staff functions.

CONSTRUCTION SUPERVISION

Designers supervise, manage, and review the components of a project and help with decision-making. Interior designers are often hired to act as liaisons between the contractor and the client. Sometimes, they are responsible for hiring other consultants and contractors.

CORPORATE CAMPUS DESIGN

The corporate campus promotes efficiency and expresses the mission of a company through design tailored to meet the specific needs of that company. The designer creates a total environment. Campuses can include administration buildings, training centers, manufacturing or production facilities, and fitness centers. Some require space that can be leased to support companies.

CORPORATE IN-HOUSE DESIGN

The staff interior designer for a corporation is responsible for maintaining its design identity. The designer may initiate and complete the design or hire design consultants on major projects, as well as act as a liaison between outside consultants and the firm.

COSMETIC DENTISTRY OFFICE DESIGN

The emergence of cosmetic dentistry has brought new challenges to the design of the dental office. The office must blend the professional medical requirements of dentistry with fashion and beauty to create effective and visually pleasing sur-roundings. The client who pays for cosmetic dentistry services is usually very conscious of design and detail.

COUNTRY CLUB DESIGN

These spaces combine aspects of residential and commer-cial design. The buildings must conform to area regulations and codes for fire, safety, labor, and industry. They must encourage proprietary feelings among the membership but must also give the staff the tools to run programs with time and financial efficiency. Facilities may include indoor swimming pools, ball courts, gyms, locker rooms, restaurants, and areas for business meetings and socializing.

DENTAL OFFICE DESIGN

This is a highly engineered segment of the medical field; the design specialist must have an understanding of the mechanics as well as the antiseptic and medical aspects of dentistry. The dental profession has exerted the effort to develop business management techniques and to improve time-use to make dentistry more efficient and professional. Space design for dental offices is an integral part of the new dentistry.

DESIGN COORDINATION

A design coordinator works directly with the client to define the client's wishes and takes the information to a design specialist. The design coordinator must be able to get along with the design professional—understanding his or her artistic attitude and approaches—but also understand and work close-ly with the client. This person is responsible for bringing the specialist and the client together in a productive way. It takes extensive knowledge of the field to be able to create such a bond. With today's global communication systems, design coordination will become a great specialty.

DESIGN FOR CHILDREN

Environment affects a child's behavior; there is a body of research indicating that what stimulates a child is not what stimulates an adult. Spaces for children must be adaptable because children change and grow so rapidly. These spaces include every place a child might use: doctors' offices, libraries, schools, and retail spaces—not just bedrooms.

The children of today are very demanding clients. They are very aware of multimedia experiences and have high expectations. Many children are also well traveled and want to be in spaces that are very special.

DESIGN FOR IN-HOME MEDICAL CARE

At one time, patients with chronic, debilitating illnesses were confined to hospital wards, but the trend today is toward in-home care. Not only do these patients enjoy the comforts of home, but they also are at less risk of acquiring new infections when their immunities are low. This specialty means more than just installing a hospital bed. The residential space must be adapted to meet geriatric, orthopedic, or other medical requirements of both patients and caregivers.

DESIGN FOR VISION AND/OR HEARING IMPAIRMENTS

The number of people affected with vision or hearing impairments grows each year in proportion to the aging of the population. More than 60 percent of people in the workforce today have some hearing loss, and probably a much larger percentage have some vision impairment. People are becoming more aware of vision and hearing problems as well as of the increased technology available to resolve them. There are successful applications for every situation, from residences to theaters.

DISPLAY AND EXHIBIT DESIGN

Retailers, wholesalers, specialty shops, museums, and all types of public spaces can use display and exhibit design to sell products as well as ideas. These displays may be permanent or built for travel. They must make an impact but also be easy to set up and take down.

ENERGY CONSERVATION DESIGN

An energy specialist advises on energy-efficient products and space planning for better use of energy. This may include solar design, adapting existing structures or developing new ones, or finding fresh uses for traditional products and appropriate uses for new ones.

ERGONOMIC DESIGN

Ergonomic design is the science that relates people to the way they use things. It's engineering science based on the physical needs of the human body. Factors considered are the body's measurements, human sensory capacities, comfort, bodily functions, safety, and emotional satisfaction.

ESTATE MANAGEMENT

Owners need a knowledgeable person to secure their investments. A trained designer is usually part of the design team, acting as the owner's representative in procurement and handling issues with contractors and artisans. After working on the property, estate managers are qualified to update and maintain the property, furnishings, and art objects; prepare operations manuals; establish budgets; and handle all financial issues. Estate managers hire and train appropriate staff, oversee inventories, and do party planning. This position requires designers with background and sophistication.

FACILITIES MANAGEMENT

The person or department responsible for the physical management of a facility coordinates purchasing, repairs, and maintenance. Facilities managers act as liaisons between the firm's executives and the consulting designers, architects, and engineers.

FACTORY/PRODUCTION CONSULTING

This specialty includes traffic control and design to improve safety and increase productivity (see ergonomic design). The emphasis is on keeping the environment stimulating, so workers stay alert, are productive, and are able to handle the machinery and equipment safely.

FAUX FINISHES AND STENCILING

Faux finishes and stenciling has become a vital and growing decorative element since the 1980s. A fine arts or interior design degree is not essential for this type of work, but either helps in translating a client's desires into reality. Tools to create faux-finishing effects are available at every hardware store and in most hardware departments. Though books on these subjects are many—making the art understandable and desirable to the general public—most clients would rather hire a specialist than attempt faux finishing themselves.

FENG SHUI

The ancient Chinese art of placement is considered the mother of natural sciences. Harmony and balance are the goals. A feng shui practitioner serves in the multiple roles of healer, therapist, cleric, business consultant, financial advisor, and matchmaker. The concepts are drawn from Tibetan, Chinese Buddhist, and folk wisdom.

FORENSIC CONSULTING

This specialty was created by the litigious times we live in. When a product is made or used incorrectly and results in injury or death, a forensic designer may be consulted by attorneys. In addition to expertise in ergonomics and product construction, the forensic designer must also be familiar with court terminology and the correct way to testify. This field requires not only training but a special personality that holds up well under pressure.

FUNERAL HOME DESIGN

The funeral home must comfort and support people at an emotionally vulnerable time. It includes personal meeting areas for family viewing and chapel spaces that must be visually pleasing as well as practical. There are presentation and financial aspects to consider, as well as the appropriate physical supports for heavy objects and space for behind-the-scenes management.

FURNITURE DESIGN

Interior design and industrial design must be blended for good product design. The interior designer knows where the furniture goes and how it is used; the industrial designer knows construction techniques.

FURNITURE MANAGEMENT

The furniture manager handles all the purchasing documents, usually for a commercial project, as well as all the bidding through to the final installation. This person is very much like a project manager on a construction project. It's a role many interior designers are very qualified to handle.

GERIATRIC DESIGN

As our society grays, design for the mature market gains in recognition. Retirement centers, nursing homes, even condominiums are designed to meet the physical, psychological, and cultural needs of older people. It's not just a case of dealing with illness and infirmity; it means acknowledging the pleasures of life and the opportunities still available. Older people are no longer simply "old." They act—and usually like to be treated—as if they are young.

GREENHOUSE DESIGN

At one time, greenhouses were simply for plants. Now they are incorporated into residential and commercial spaces that also accommodate people. Depending on the climate required for a given greenhouse, the design can involve controlling temperature, light, and humidity. Insulating elements and the design atmosphere are other factors. Manufacturers consult interior designers on the design of greenhouse components; some designers have made this their specialty.

HARD SURFACE FLOORING DESIGN

Designing this type of flooring requires knowledge of color trends, as well as a working knowledge of the properties of wood, ceramics, marble, vinyl, and other appropriate materials. In fact, there are so many hard-surfaced floors and flooring products that each one requires individual specialists.

HARDWARE DESIGN

The work of interior and industrial designers enhances the functional and decorative effects of knobs, hinges, handles, or any hardware for use in buildings and on furniture. The demand is increasing for beautifully sculptured, handsomely crafted hardware.

HEALTH AND FITNESS CLUB DESIGN

Personal fitness became important in the 1980s. Health clubs are not just places to exercise, but meeting spots for people with similar goals and interests. Athletic, aerobic, and recreational facilities of all sorts are proliferating. Keeping the facilities safe, convenient, and appropriate to their specific sports is involved enough that some designers have made it their specialty. Health and fitness club design has some aspects in common with country club design. As trends change, these spaces must be redesigned to meet the new needs.

HISTORIC PRESERVATION

Historic preservation demands technical and scientific knowledge, and an ability and willingness to research small details. What colors, materials, and wallcovering were in use when the building was created? Technology has given us the means to determine the original colors (they are often garish when compared to the more subtle shades we are accustomed to seeing today). What hardware is appropriate? How historically accurate does the client want the building to be? Some people want the interiors to be absolutely authentic with no substitutions or modifications, and will hide the electricity or do without it. We can assign precise dates to furniture. The body of knowledge continues to grow.

HOME OFFICE DESIGN

The home office is a space tailored to the way an individual works. Working with people who have been on the corporate scene for many years and now want home offices can be exciting. The office may be small—incorporated into part of an apartment or bedroom—or it may be larger than any executive office in a corporate building. Quite often, the office contains all the bells and whistles of a commercial space, along with all the comforts of home, plus a few indulgences.

HOME THEATER

Home theater design is in great demand. This area of work requires extensive technical and audiovisual knowledge, and knowledge of many different aspects of design. Not only do these rooms need to be very luxurious and comfortable—with the ability to access any cable or satellite system with the push of a button—but the clients also expect sound to be perfect and the picture to be crisp and clear. The home theater has become one of the most expensive rooms of a residence.

HOSPITAL DESIGN

Today, some areas in hospitals have such complex technical requirements that designers with a particular specialty have international practices. Subspecialties proliferate. Some designers do only emergency rooms and intensive care units, while others design patient and visitor areas. Some designers combine both. Hospitals are changing dramatically and quickly to support new systems of medicine, causing hospital designers to put aside most of their traditional systems and work with System Technology, a new and very demanding set of guidelines. Fortunately, as a result hospitals are much more user-friendly. Insurance and legal requirements, along with the search for cost-effective products and services, place demands and constraints on the design. It is highly unlikely that a specialist in hospital design would also work on a nursing-home project; the demands are very different.

HOSPITALITY DESIGN

This field can range from a bed-and-breakfast to a large conference center. Some conference centers are practically cities in themselves. Hospitality design encompasses luxury spaces for community and celebration, as well as functional accommodations. Designers may specialize in restaurant dining halls, training centers and convention spaces, guest rooms, lobbies, or corridors.

HOTEL DESIGN

Many products are shown and sold through hotels. Clients have the opportunity to spend the night testing out furniture—including the mattress, bedding, and other appointments. They can sit on them, sleep on them, and really experience them; then they have the opportunity to purchase many of the items directly. Designers are working with hospitality companies to gain this exposure.

HOUSEBOAT DESIGN

Houseboats are, in essence, both residential and commercial structures. There is a tremendous amount of technical engineering required to keep them afloat as well as to meet health and safety requirements. Houseboats can be three, four, or five stories high and provide sizeable living and work spaces.

HUMAN FACTORS

Human factors deal with personal performance in work or personal spaces. Designers who specialize in this field often consult with owners and other design specialists to incorporate human concerns into standard and special-need spaces.

INTERIOR LANDSCAPING

Plants add a natural quality to even the most static environment. This field requires knowledge of landscaping and botany in order to place plants where they are suitable. It may include contracting to provide maintenance and design changes for seasonal updates and plant health. While greenhouses are primarily used to keep plants healthy and growing, interior plantscaping is an increasingly important component of a building's atmosphere. Design factors include temperature, light, and humidity control.

INTERNET RESOURCING AND SELLING

This has become a major specialty within the last few years. In fact, Internet selling is now one of the most profitable specialties in the field. Many designers do most of their purchasing through the Internet or act as consultants to other designers to help resource the products and materials. Other designers use the Internet as a vehicle to trade in the existing furniture of clients so they can buy new furniture. With trading, clients are more inclined to update or upgrade. eBay and Craigslist are two popular sites. eBay is an excellent vehicle to increase business. It can also be a profitable independent career for designers living anywhere in the world.

JOURNALISM

Through writing, designers can make our work more understandable to people inside and outside the field. Designers can educate the public through columns and articles on design for newspapers and magazines, and, more recently, on television as well. Writing is a special skill, as is the ability to relate on camera. Some people with design education have chosen design journalism but only after intensive efforts to learn these additional skills. If these skills do not come easily, designers who need to produce books and articles would do well to collaborate with a writer. This may be a more effective use of their time.

KENNEL DESIGN

In the competitive world of breeding pedigreed pets, space design for each species is a serious business. You must understand animals and their needs. In kennels, there are areas for grooming and training, food preparation and nutrition, as well as testing. Maintenance and health care are prime concerns.

KITCHEN DESIGN

The kitchen is often one of the most expensive parts of the house. Most equipment is unabashedly brand new. There are also historic designs infused with new technology. Scientific and artistic detail goes into the design and planning of components for residential and contract-use kitchens. The designer must have a complete knowledge of currently available products, as well as the dietary requirements of the users.

The National Kitchen and Bath Association (NKBA) has created a curriculum that is presented by numerous design schools throughout the country. This program accredits designers in kitchen design.

LAW OFFICE DESIGN

Law offices have many features in common with residences. A designer who is skilled in residential work may be excellent at designing them. Image, cost, and work efficiency are important considerations. An environment that supports legal professionals, visiting clients and consultants provides visual and acoustical privacy. Law offices now incorporate highly technical equipment, as well as areas for personal interaction.

LEEDS (LEADERSHIP IN ENERGY AND ENVIRONMENT DESIGN SYSTEM)

Clients are looking not only for long-lasting products but for buildings that will last many years. They want buildings to have flexibility, so they aren't just designed for today's purposes but for long term and environmentally friendly use. A sustainability person has to be knowledgeable in LEEDS and qualified as a LEEDS specialist. This individual must understand flexibility of use in building design.

LIBRARY DESIGN

Libraries are individual and specialized, catering to local needs. A library in a county seat will be different from one on Wall Street. Libraries need space planning and marketing, with special attention to lighting and acoustics. Many libraries have exhibit areas or function rooms. They are true multimedia environments, lending books, videocassettes, art, and music. Electrical demands have increased greatly with the advent of computers, which are used for card catalogs, periodical indexes, and subject-dedicated databases. In addition, spaces for extensive personal libraries are enjoying a comeback. Personal libraries are no longer just for English country homes.

LICENSING

Many designers license their names to a product line. The designer can style or develop a product or merely endorse it. This is a growing field encompassing wallcoverings, upholstery textiles, bed linens, tabletop china, and just about everything that can be used in interior spaces. Today, very fine designers plan projects for inexpensive merchandise. Licensing fees are based on volume, and work on easily available consumer goods becomes very lucrative. Although some licensers are used principally for their names, most designers actually contribute to the design of products for widely divergent markets.

LIGHTING DESIGN

Lighting, both natural and artificial, is a strong and important element used for design, drama, ecology, and, of course, function. Scale, structure, engineering, and knowledge of the end user are critical components of good lighting design, as are the technical requirements and codes for specific projects.

LIGHTING FIXTURE DESIGN

In any space, the human eye goes to the windows and lighting fixtures. Scale, structure, engineering, and knowledge of the end use are critical components of good lighting-fixture design—the design of actual fixtures. This specialty requires some training in industrial design.

LITURGICAL DESIGN

Churches, synagogues and mosques are not just monuments, but living centers that actively serve the community. Some offer recreation areas for children. These buildings are used for social events, theater productions, educational lectures, and community activities. Of course, each religion has its own design requirements; the designer must know and understand the liturgy.

MANUFACTURE OF IN-HOUSE DESIGN

Manufacturers have staff designers who work, not on design, but on merchandising. In order to promote sales, many contract office furniture manufacturers offer interior design services at little or no cost to the end user. Designers, especially interior designers, work directly for manufacturers to help align products to the needs of today's design public.

MANUFACTURER REPRESENTATION

This sales position is the link between the manufacturer and interior designer. Some of the best manufacturers' representatives are former interior designers or dealers. They understand the product, know how to sell it, and appreciate what interior designers want. Within assigned territories, manufacturers' reps call on designers, providing catalogs, assisting in specification preparation, and writing purchase orders.

MARINE DESIGN

This specialty requires extensive knowledge of fire codes, marine standards, regulations, weights, and materials. Many products must be made specifically for marine use. Marine design encompasses all sizes of ships and boats, from working boats to cruise liners with the size and complexity of small villages. The design demands range from stripped-down—where every inch must have more than one use—to extravagant—with swimming pools, shops, ballrooms, and health spas. The designer deals with physical, psychological, and ergonomic issues as well. There are fewer restrictions—sometimes none at all—on smaller crafts for personal use.

MARKETING

Marketing specialists work in many parts of the market and with the end users as well as designers. They represent design firms to the end users. Marketing specialists develop and position design firms with appropriate clients. Some designers are better at design work than selling, so the need for and value of this specialty is well recognized and compensated.

MEDICAL CENTER DESIGN

Medical centers differ from typical hospitals in that they usually don't have intensive care and critical care units. Medical centers are usually designed for outpatient surgery or equipped with all the various physicians and support personnel for a particular specialty. In some cases medical centers look like shopping centers, with different types of design than hospitals.

Some doctors are designing centers to fit their own specialties. The medical field is changing so rapidly that some facilities are not even completed before major changes must be made. Outpatient care has expanded so dramatically that it has changed the profile of every medical institution. Medicine is advancing dramatically, so we can look forward to much more work in this area.

MEDICAL OFFICE DESIGN

Every medical specialty requires special equipment, as well as appropriate space planning, traffic patterns, and storage management. Today's specialties use such an intensive array of high-tech equipment that office plans require total restructuring every few years. A complete understanding of the medical procedures and equipment, legal aspects, codes, and aseptic demands is needed. There are extreme challenges in this area because the equipment in even the largest office is so imposing, and HIPAA (Health Insurance Portability and Accountability Act) regulations require every office to make major changes.

MEDICAL SPAS

Medical spas encompass the offices of plastic surgeons and dermatologists for all types of skin treatments. These facilities require a considerable amount of equipment. The

214

knowledge of both the processes and treatments offered as well as of the necessary equipment is essential for this design specialty. The medical spa may also include cosmetic dentistry, anti-aging systems, hydrotherapy, and many other forms of massage and exercise treatments.

MODULAR PREFABRICATED DESIGN

This area of the building industry is growing rapidly. A high level of quality with skilled engineering can be achieved through prefabricated design. Understanding the requirements of building and delivery is critical. It's not just price but also quality that's relevant here. You can construct a much better product more cost-effectively by building standard components under controlled factory conditions. Factory-built housing or modular complexes for other purposes also come with guarantees, something not available in on-site construction. Modular prefab construction is usually most practical when you're building a hundred or more similar units. The designer creates a standard, builds a sample, checks all the details, confirms with the client, and analyzes the finished product. When all has been approved, several hundred units are built. These units ship well over water, which can be a construction advantage when placing large complexes on deserted islands, where there are very few construction trades.

MODEL HOME FURNISHING

Model home furnishing can be handled by an independent designer, who may also specify the architectural details of the interior to be purchased and installed by another contractor, or by companies dedicated to furnishing model homes. There are also companies who grant all of the furniture, accessories, and appointments to builders to use for several months or a year. At the end of that period, the companies retrieve the furniture to reuse in another project.

Model home design can be a promotional tool for design firms. In some areas, interior designers pay contractors or developers for the privilege of working on their models. The work may encompass all the interior architectural details, lighting, fixture specifications, and hard and soft furnishings. The furnishings are often sold with the home. In other instances, contractors consider this work part of the presentation of the home and will hire designers or lease furnishings, or both.

MURAL PAINTING

A number of mural artists are interior designers with fine arts backgrounds. They first paint a miniature for the client, then execute the full-size product on canvas or directly on a wall. This art form has become very prominent. The demand is increasing to create a new specialty: hand-painted walls.

MUSEUM DESIGN

At one time, only people with backgrounds in history or art history worked in museums. However, museums today provide many opportunities for interior designers to work on exhibits, promotions, and community projects. Because the preservation of artifacts is as important as the display, understanding the effects of humidity and lighting on artifacts is important. Interior designers may work directly for museums or be employed by consulting firms that specialize in museum work.

NURSING HOME DESIGN

As health care changes, so do the codes, systems, regulations, and requirements. Nursing homes now cater not only to senior citizens but to young people who have short-term needs, such as those who live alone or have no one to care for them but require care for a limited time. Elements to consider in the design of nursing or convalescent homes include the probable length of the stay and the special equipment patients will need. Changes in medicine make many facilities obsolete before they are five years old, so it is important to plan for change.

OFFICE DESIGN

While commercial and home offices have elements in common, the home office is usually for one or two people. Commercial office design requires knowledge of high-tech equipment, as well as an understanding of management and office production. The term "commercial office" may still suggest open-plan offices. However, companies vary; hence, they need different types of design. In general, these spaces are designed for large groups of people working together in a cooperative and productive fashion. The space must accommodate many different disciplines with varying needs.

PARK AND GARDEN DESIGN

Municipal and other parks need safety, effective traffic patterns, management systems, and efficiency. Designers may be called on to develop unique signage, or to design fixtures or service areas: food service, restrooms, and souvenir shops. The emphasis is on getting people to come back often, especially if the park is for-profit. Parks are also hubs for many other environments, such as residential complexes or campuses for education, hospitality, medicine or business.

PASSENGER TRAIN AND BUS DESIGN

The interiors of passenger trains and buses must be designed for the comfort and safety of the travelers. The interiors also need to be attractive. Passenger trains and buses of today are so different from those of the past. They incorporate much more technology and are more pleasant environments.

PATIO AND OUTDOOR FURNITURE DESIGN

Some designers are now specializing only in patio and outdoor furniture design. They style the area for clients and change it periodically according to the season. They arrange to restore and store furniture over the winter months, so in the spring everything is in good order and clients have no maintenance problems. When the client is having a party, the designer will style the area specifically for that event so the patio is always at its best.

PARTY AND BALL DESIGN

Designers organize and orchestrate parties and balls for corporations, charities, and other organizations. Entertainment and celebration require an appropriate atmosphere. It is not enough just to put people into a ballroom for so many hours; they want fantasies brought to life. The competition among charities is intense. The donors have been in every hotel many times. If you cannot show them something different, they are not interested.

PHOTOGRAPHIC SET DESIGN

These specialists work with manufacturers and advertising agencies to create settings designed to sell products. They maintain an inventory of props and backgrounds, spend weeks creating and building a set, then tear it down immediately after photographing it. Successful photographic set design requires an understanding of what photographs well and what does not, as well as what can be faked.

PLUMBING FIXTURE DESIGN

To design sinks, lavatories, bathtubs, and spas, the designer must have training and a special interest in sculpture. Sometimes the specialist will be asked to recolor or redesign an existing line, but more often, the project means creating new forms. Fixture manufacturers may revive the shapes of antiques or items from the Orient, reworking them to meet today's plumbing standards. The day of strictly utilitarian bathroom fixtures is gone.

PRISON DESIGN

State and local governments are turning to private companies for help in constructing prisons, which are then leased back to the government. Some organizations, such as Volunteers of America, actually operate the prisons. Prison design is a specialty in the midst of change. Social scientists suggest that new prisons should not just house prisoners but help to rehabilitate them.

PRIVACY

Privacy is a major issue in almost every type of environment and design today, from public buildings to private residences. Privacy consultants have a design background, complemented with sound engineering training.

PRODUCT DESIGN

Opportunities in the field of product design are as numerous as the products themselves. Designers can make vital contributions in helping manufacturers find and develop products that are wanted, function well, and suit the environments they will be used in. Designers have a hand in almost every product available today.

PRODUCT DISPLAY

Interior designers have traditionally designed store windows and product displays, but never has this type of design been brought to the level of so refined and sophisticated an art form as recently. A strong merchandising approach often permits unlimited budgets, which encourage a free range of ideas.

PRODUCT EVALUATION

Hiring designers to evaluate products for design quality, practicality, and marketability is a sound investment for manufacturers.

PRODUCT MARKETING

Interior designers assist with marketing products by developing ways to use the products. They are well qualified to assist in product design development as a complement to the manufacturer's design staff. Consulting interior designers can help maintain a firm's position in the marketplace.

PROFESSIONAL OR PROMOTIONAL ORGANIZATIONS

Trade and professional organizations often hire interior designers as spokespersons or interpreters to build links between the product group and designer or client. The designers' skill and knowledge can strengthen that relationship. Designers understand the needs of the end user as well as the multitude of design disciplines involved.

PROJECT MANAGEMENT

Project management can be as simple as handling interior design development for one's own firm, or as complex as running a project under a turnkey proposition. It requires complete understanding of various crafts.

PROXEMICS

Proxemics is the physical, psychological, and cultural impact of space on people. A consultant in this field evaluates any type of interior space that affects human behavior or where there is social interaction. Private-use spaces such as residences can gain tremendously from this specialty.

PSYCHIATRIC CARE FACILITY DESIGN

While many of the codes in the psychiatric care facilities are the same as in other medical facilities, the type of therapy practice determines the design response. Use, practicality, privacy, safety, and ease of maintenance are prime concerns.

PUBLIC RELATIONS

Interior designers with strong communications skills may choose to draw media attention to the work of other designers rather than run a design practice of their own. Some act as liaisons between manufacturers, designers, and end users.

PURCHASING

The designer may act as a purchasing agent for large companies, reviewing and testing products, then negotiating and ordering the furnishings. Purchasing agents or procurement companies can get better prices for individual design firms than the firms could get on their own.

REAL ESTATE DEVELOPMENT

A knowledge of space, its uses, and its potential for change has given many interior designers an edge in real estate sales and development. Some designers assist developers by restructuring and designing buildings for turnkey or development projects. In some states, interior designers need a realtor's license to be recognized and compensated for their contributions. In others, interior designers are a part of a real estate development firm.

REAL ESTATE UPGRADING

Build a better home, please the client, and sell. These are the objectives in design upgrading for luxury development homes. Many experienced designers have moved into this specialty. There is opportunity for creative design, and this specialty pays very well.

RENDERING

CAD can do a lot, but there is nothing like a beautiful hand rendering. Rendering is a special art requiring knowledge of graphics, fine art, and design. A good presentation is vital. Many design firms—even small ones—hire good renderers, either staff or freelance. Fees can run into the thousands of dollars.

RESIDENTIAL DESIGN

At one time, residential design was the most prevalent design specialty and also the most lucrative. It requires knowledge of human behavior within living spaces, understanding, an ability to communicate with people, and respect for clients. Generally, people hire residential designers whose tastes and communications skills are similar to their own.

RESORT DESIGN

Resorts are wonderful vacation places for hosting many types of activities, from a very luxurious and indulging spa, to the experiential resort that boasts everything from extreme sports to tame activities, such as listening to music or pursuing other specialized interests. Resorts are found all over the country in many environments. They generally have many unique features. Resort designers are often experts in a particular specialty as well as in hospitality design. They are very aware of the unique issues in designing a space that has both living and activity areas.

RESTAURANT DESIGN

There is room for design in every restaurant, from the fast-food stands in malls, to local eateries, to establishments for gracious dining. Knowledge of all design disciplines as well as of food management is essential.

RESTAURANT KITCHEN DESIGN

This requires knowledge of kitchen equipment and the know-how to adapt the space and tools it will hold to the preferences of individual restaurateurs. Kitchen specialists work independently or for equipment suppliers. Kitchens for country clubs, educational facilities, and large commercial restaurants are typical projects.

RETAIL AND SPECIALTY SELLING

Selling is part of every design practice. Some designers have found it more lucrative to own, manage, or work for retail and specialty stores. Designers make good salespeople, especially in design-related areas, because they understand how to use a product and can demonstrate for clients. Interior designers may help develop a product mix for a specific store. This often means creating a design package to be sold by other people. It also can mean working with a group of artists to market their work.

RETAIL STORE DESIGN

This popular specialty requires skill in image development and marketing, knowledge of traffic patterns and security, and concern for financial return on space. Custom fixturing is often part of the design. The designer may customize local spaces for national chains or work with individual storeowners.

SECURITY CONSULTING

Security must be built into every part of a building's design today; it's not just something supplementary. Security incorporates many different types of systems, such as screening and the use of other cameras and devices that permit different types of monitoring. Security consultants are now so specialized that some deal only in educational institutions. Others work in federal and state buildings or office buildings; yet others work in residential spaces.

SET DESIGN

Many interior designers started in set design; others expanded their practices to include it. Although this is a unionized profession, there are still some opportunities. Set design for movies, theater, dance, and opera is a different world. You build for show, not to last. You design everything to be seen from a certain perspective. The size and design of the theater—whether it is a proscenium or a theater-in-the-round—affect the placement of furniture and props. The director's vision of the production is critical to the choice of furnishings.

SHOP-AT-HOME SERVICES

At-home shopping is powerful. There are extremely successful firms that specialize in this service. Some stock a van or truck with a coordinated line of pictures, accessories, pillows, and draperies. They distribute their products to representatives or franchise owners. Even very sophisticated firms are finding ways to bring products to the home. If you can show clients a product sample in their own space, very often you can sell it.

SHOPPING MALL DESIGN

This is large-scale marketing. Each store in a mall must contribute to the total mall concept, which ranges from discount to luxury. Each mall promotes a different lifestyle or environment. Designers may work directly for mall owners to coordinate all mall activities and designs. They may also work with individual retailers and in the common areas. The mall of today must allow space for entertainment and other activities. It must be an experience in itself, not just a place to shop.

SHOWROOM DESIGN

In Manhattan, Rome, Paris, London, and in every small city in the United States, showroom designs and presentations account for an amazingly high dollar figure. The primary job of the showroom is to sell a product. The beauty of the showroom is a question of taste, but whether it works can be measured.

SPAS/SKIN SPAS

This major trend requires many specific design considerations. Cosmetic approaches include skin treatments, facials, and therapeutic massage. The demands of this specialty are so great that many designers work in this area exclusively.

SPACESHIP AND ROCKET DESIGN

This is the ultimate challenge in ergonomic design—every inch must count. Many consumer products have been developed as a result of studies done for spaceship design. Designers who have worked for NASA have taught us many things we can use in general work.

SOLAR DESIGN

Design for solar buildings is not just a matter of solar collection but of coordinating solar and environmental concerns with human needs. Energy efficiency, sun control, sunlight-resistant materials, and insulation are key.

STADIUM AND ARENA DESIGN

While architects and engineers are most often involved with shaping the spaces, interior designers are consulted on public areas, private salons, dining areas, kitchens, service areas, and even the choice of seating. This specialty has aspects in common with theater, restaurant, and store design. Today's stadiums and arenas are expensive and luxurious but also must incorporate safety and security as primary concerns.

STORAGE DESIGN

Planned storage is an essential design element. Storage specialists catalog clients' storable objects and materials, then plan for growth. Custom storage can range from making tiny drawers for accommodating contact lenses to developing automated filing areas for offices. Good storage means placing things in convenient locations near where they'll be used, and putting lesser-used items in less accessible places. Since storage is generally an engineering process within each of our disciplines, a designer will usually specialize in a particular discipline of storage design, such as residential, legal, or medical offices, or other types of commercial space.

STYLING FOR PHOTOGRAPHY

Designers team with photographers to make interior spaces work better in photographs. This involves moving furniture to show the room to advantage and accessorizing the space. Very few interior designers and architects understand how to stage their own work for good photography.

TABLETOP DISPLAY DESIGN

These designers often do display work in addition, but most design firms have a tabletop specialist who shows clients how to coordinate their tables and food services with the overall design of their home. Restaurants and department and specialty stores use tabletop display to sell food and other products. Clients today expect both drama and practicality.

TELECONFERENCE CENTER DESIGN

Teleconference centers exist not only in large corporations but also in community centers and occasionally in apartment complexes. This discipline specifies the shape of the room, lighting, choice and placement of furnishings, and even the teleconferencing equipment. Sight lines, light and sound control, and audibility are prime concerns.

TELEVISION DESIGN

There are presently forty-three different television shows with interior design as the subject. This has become a major focus in entertainment. Television designers may do all of the preparation as well as the on-camera work. Many of these designers also have a background in theater.

TENANT DEVELOPMENT SERVICES

Interior designers work with landlords and developers to coordinate interior spaces for homes, apartments, and commercial offices. They may devise color schemes and layouts or may only ensure that the work of other designers coordinates with what exists in these buildings.

TEXTILE DESIGN

These interior designers have special knowledge of textiles, design rugs, fabrics, and wallcoverings. This combined discipline creates products that are appropriate, distinctive, and easy to use.

TRAINING CENTER DESIGN

Education takes place in more places than schools. Corporate training centers are found in office buildings; smaller firms use hotel meeting rooms or convention centers. Special demands include adaptable lighting, audiovisual equipment, and attention to acoustics and sight lines.

TRANSIT CENTER DESIGN

Airport, train, and bus terminals have almost become living environments for some people. Interior designers are called on to enhance people movement—to entertain travelers and accommodate their needs with airport shops, small conference areas, VIP clubs, and cocktail lounges. There is not much one can't do in transit centers these days, from banking, to seeing a podiatrist, to hiring a secretary. Transit centers are now like small cities in the range of services they offer the daily commuter, as well as the traveler who may have a layover of many hours. Chicago's O'Hare Airport has a laser show. Some centers offer college courses while others have educational displays. There is usually a church or chapel.

Today's security demands have also changed many facets of transit centers. These areas will continue to reflect a significant demand for innovative design.

TURNKEY SERVICES

A team of designers, contractors, and vendors takes a project from a client's desire to a completed, move-in, ready-to-use building. The client deals only with one person or firm, agreeing to the terms and costs of the total project. This is a very efficient and cost-effective way of working. All the client needs to do is turn the key and open the door.

UNDERGROUND HABITATION

Because the temperature underground is a constant 55 degrees Fahrenheit, underground space has become a practical and appropriate area for living and working. Many computer centers, for example, are located underground. Yet, this field of design is relatively underdeveloped.

UNIVERSAL DESIGN

Universal design is not just designing for the physically handicapped; it is intended to be useful for all. Spaces are often designed for multiple purposes so they can function well for many different people and reasons. Universal design is becoming standard among many building specifications today, to ensure that the structure is user-friendly and convenient for all.

VACATION HOME DESIGN

Second homes are big business, but they often must be designed as turnkey projects because the clients are involved elsewhere. This market is growing. For some clients, the vacation home is a place to indulge in an opulence they would not feel comfortable expressing in other areas of their lives.

VASTU

This is an ancient practice from India that has been in use for more than a thousand years. The objectives are to achieve harmony, maximize the flow of energy, and make the home a retreat where we can recuperate from the stresses of the world. Vastu uses a systematic approach to building and design. Practitioners believe our homes play an important part in helping us achieve our purpose and goals in life.

WALLCOVERING DESIGN

Many interior designers focus on wallcoverings, drawing on their expertise with color, pattern direction, and scale. The field demands production and design expertise as well as an understanding of current trends.

WALL FINISHES

Marbling, fresco, and textured finishes—some of which have not been seen for centuries—are again in demand. This specialty is no longer limited to historic restoration work; commercial and residential clients also are requesting novel wall finishes.

WAYFINDING

Wayfinding involves signage but also many other aspects of interior design. It means designing a space, building, or complex that's easy for people to move around in. Finding one's way becomes natural rather than complicated and confusing. This specialty first became popular in hospitals but is now relevant to almost every large complex. People want to be able to find what they're interested in easily, whether on a campus, in a conference center, a hotel, or any other complex.

WINDOW TREATMENT DESIGN

Draperies, shades, louver drapes, valances, cornices, and a broad spectrum of other treatments make up this specialty. Insulation, ventilation, light control, and energy conservation are all a part of today's window treatment design.

CHAPTER 15

DESIGN YOUR CAREER

You've seen your business change many times in many ways. Some of these changes were positive. Others you wish hadn't happened. We know the value of design. We also know there are different opportunities for us today than there were previously.

LOVE WHAT YOU DO

If you want to be successful, you have to love what you do. Making a life is as important as making a living. These assertions come from a book called *Success Built to Last: Creating a Life that Matters* by Jerry Porras, Stewart Emery, and Mark Thompson.[1] The book excels at explaining that passion for work is dominant in almost all successful people. Successful people have another thing in common—great integrity. They really believe in what they're doing and know that their belief makes a difference. They're very stubborn and stick to their values with great passion.

One of the most difficult things in life is finding what's meaningful to us. Once we do, it's important to really follow that path. This isn't something we can copy from someone else. It's something we know when we find it. If we follow that "something" faithfully, it leads to incredible success.

Design work requires a lot of determination and skill. We can't work at anything we don't have great skill at. There's no substitute for knowledge, talent, and experience. This is extremely important in all phases of our careers. We also want to be sure that we're making new mistakes, not repeating the same ones, and that when we're persistent, we are persistent about the right things. This makes us exceptional. Successful designers have a definite direction, and everyone around them understands their direction. They also work at building relationships that will last forever. How long do you keep a client? As I've said, that depends on who lives longer.

REINVENTION

Reinvention is an important part of what we do. We need to keep reinventing our companies to keep them exciting for us, as well as for our clients. Madonna is a great example of a star who has been very successful by constantly reinventing herself. She anticipates cultural changes and the behavior patterns of her audience. Then she reinvents herself to appeal to them. We need to consider the directions of our market and reinvent our design firms to stay ahead of them.

To design your new company for the twenty-first century, look at what appear to be small trends or interesting issues. Review them seriously. What do they mean to your future market? Are they beginning to be serious trends? Look at everything you've been doing in the past. Is there a way you can do it better or differently? What can you do to improve on it? Don't be afraid of going that extra step. Some of your clients may appear too "far out there." They may be the ones who notice where things are going.

Look at your resources. Are they really meeting your needs today? Often we continue to buy from people because they've been faithful to us. But are they up to date? Are they really where you need to be? Maybe you need to consider changing your sources or adding some new ones.

Consider underserved parts of the market. By specializing in a particular area, or serving an area no one else is taking seriously, you can develop a wonderful new market.

REDESIGNING YOUR BUSINESS

The challenge now is to redesign your business into a more vital entity—one that fulfills your need to create but also meets the needs of the market today and tomorrow.

You need to keep a history of your business; your mission statement; and your answers to the hopes, dreams, and reality questionnaire. You may have done this before. Do it again—you'll be surprised what you can learn from this exercise. Start now, because you cannot redesign your business without this information.

Your first step is to list your accomplishments and abilities, both as a firm and individually. Make lists of your successes and values. What's your business goal? This is your mission statement. Then dream a little. What would you really like to be doing in five years? Do your dreams fit with the realities of your business? What can you do to make your dreams achievable? You do this for your clients; now it's your chance to design your firm to fit you and your team's talents and abilities.

What do you need to do to complete your mission statement? You have defined your abilities, what you do, and what you want to do in the next five years. What steps should you plan to take? In order to achieve your goals, you may need to change your staff, consultants, craftspeople, or resumes. You may need to purchase new tools or technology for your studio. You may need to develop your client base. Most likely you'll need to work on all of these.

Goals, Dreams, and Reality

To find or create the perfect job as an interior designer, it's important to have your goals and dreams in mind. Writing them down sometimes helps define them.

- What do you like to do?
- What would you like your company to do for you?
- If you could earn more money and do more of what you like, would you work for a company other than your own?
- Is your career going in the right direction?
- Who are your preferred clients?
- Do you want to find your own clients, or do you prefer someone else to do it for you?
- What income would you like to earn?
- What perks would you like to have?
- What hours would you like to work?
- What is your education and experience?

- What type of projects have you done?
- What do you have to do to fulfill your mission statement?
- What do you have to change to meet your goals?

List the changes you need and the steps that will make them a reality. Then rate the changes and steps from one to ten, as if you were designing a room. When a client has a limited budget, we go over the project, evaluating what needs to be done and how much it's going to cost. That way we can invest money where it really counts. We have to look at our businesses in the same way.

Consider the changes in the market. These are some we mentioned earlier in the book. You should be able to think of others.

- There are fewer places for consumers to see, feel, and test merchandise.
- Products are now available through many sources.
- Clients have less time for extensive shopping; convenience is essential.
- Clients are more interested in value.
- Clients want faster service.
- There are more home offices and smaller corporate spaces today than formerly.
- There is a largely untapped mature market.
- There is a huge body of information available to everyone through the Internet.

At least one of these issues should call for a change in your firm. Whether you're in contract or residential design, you'll find changes in your clients' expectations, and you must adjust the way you conduct business. What do you need to do to support your clients better?

HISTORY OF THE FIRM

Writing a history of your firm will help you understand where you are today and provide a base to build on for the future. Create a history as if you were writing a biography of your firm. You don't have to do it all at once. Jot down some of your more memorable experiences and projects. What did you learn from them? Where did you get off-track? What projects led you in new directions?

Whether you choose to write it on a computer or on a pad of paper, your firm's history is developmental. The best time to record the history of a project is when you finish it. You tend to forget details over time. This information is very valuable when you're preparing proposals for new projects or considering changes in your services.

Firm History

- Start with the history of the founders: background and education, family's socioeconomic background, the year the firm opened.
- What experience did you have when you started your firm or joined this company? What year was that?
- How did you get a sound financial base?
- Why are you in interior design?
- What are your work experience and areas of specialization?
- What type of projects have you worked on?
- List special accomplishments.

Design Career History

Record your progress with a yearly summary. If you've been in business a long time, you might want to write the history in blocks of five years. It can be as simple or as complex as you want it to be.

Your career design will need the following information.

- What jobs did you do? What did you accomplish?
- What did you learn from those jobs?
- What were your methods of working?
- Did the clients become part of your design family?
- Staff profiles.
- What resources did you use, and what do you think of them? Will you continue to use them?
- Your consultants.
- Your financial profile.

A pattern should emerge. You may find that early in your career you handled primarily small residential projects for empty nesters. Later on your practice might have concentrated on second homes or larger residential projects. Or your firm might have taken on a specialty. Some practices specializing in educational facilities began with kindergarten design but moved into middle schools when the demographics changed.

Experience and Direction

What do you want to do in the near future? The following questions will help define your direction.

- What's your image? What makes your firm unique? Ask your clients what they think.
- What kinds of projects are you qualified to do?
- What do you need to learn?
- What are your methods of working?
- What types of clients do you hope to make part of your design family?
- Do you have the right skills on staff for what you want to do?
- What consultants will your firm need?
- What kinds of resources do you need to complete projects successfully?

Career Development Worksheet

This is an annual assessment of your personal progress and what you learned as you worked on projects. At first, you may want to do a career development summary, then update it annually. Whether you're the firm's leader or an employee, just thinking about what you learned over the past year can be useful.

1. List the projects you completed or were a part of.
2. List the benefits your clients received from the firm's work and from your specific contributions.
3. Describe what you learned through working at the firm over this period.

4. Explain why you're more valuable today than you were a year ago.
5. List the new people who helped make it possible for you to work, and describe how they helped.
6. What new responsibilities or projects do you plan to take on in the next year?
7. What are your goals with this firm, and how do you plan to accomplish them?

Attach references from clients, vendors, and craftspeople as testimonials to the quality of your completed work. Include any relevant information about what you accomplished during this period.

This is the kind of information you need to plan a future for your firm, whether you do it by yourself or with a consultant. The designers in my seminars find that just the process of answering questions suggests a new direction. Filling out all the questionnaires should result in an outline for the design for your future firm. Of course, it will need fine-tuning. You'll have to revise the outline as you go along.

Your career design will show you where you've been and where you want to go. You know what you're secure with and where you should invest new energies.

COACHING

Even though you may be entirely capable of devising your own career design, consider using a consultant as a coach if you're thinking of changing or enhancing your business. The purpose of the coach/trainer is to empower design professionals to achieve higher levels of performance, greater job satisfaction, and increased profits.

A coach/trainer will help you see your firm's abilities more clearly, examine the behavioral influences of your staff and team members, and create a method for measuring progress. With the above information, your coach will determine the ratio of risk to probable gain in your course of action.

The coach should help you develop a management system appropriate to your practice. Typically, the process will include measuring systems of working, buying, marketing and selling, business development, charging, team building, and money management. Continuing education and benchmarking should also be included.

The trainer relationship should continue with weekly or biweekly interactions to ensure that the system is working and you can make necessary adjustments.

STRATEGY

Strategy is a group of integrated decisions that the leader/director of a firm or practice must make to position the business. These decisions should be firm and clearly stated so the director, staff, and your team can follow them precisely:

1. What is your present strategy?
2. How do you envision the future of your business? How has the vision changed?
3. Is your present strategy a good one?
4. What are some other options?
5. Which one of these options appeals to you the most?
6. Create a usable strategy including your mission and vision statements. This is an essential part of developing a clear direction for your business.

Interior design usually has an entrepreneurial structure headed by one person who has a group of people working with him or her. Even now that the style of business calls for increasing equalization of roles, there should be a leader or director. This is probably the best system for most businesses. It permits the business to shift and change with the environment, without cumbersome bureaucratic procedures or chaos caused by lack of leadership.

Your business strategy must include all of these components:

- Products. Define the products you're selling.
- Market. Which clients will want and need what you have to sell?

239

- Price structure. How are you going to charge?
- Service. Which services do you have to provide to bring a product to the given market?
- Sources. Which sources do you have access to? How good is your relationship with those sources? How reliable are they?
- Distribution. What will the process of distribution be? How are you going to get merchandise to your clients?
- Team. Who is on the team? Can you count on them? What part do they play in the business?
- Facility. What type of facility do you need to display and store your products? Do you need a showroom, studio, or something else? Does your type of practice demand high visibility and easy access, or could you work out of the second floor of a garage?
- Finances. What kind of capital do you need? What will your cash flow be? Where does the money come from, where does it go, and what's left in the end?
- System of operation. What type of system do you need to make your business work properly? What are your checks and balances?
- Technology. How does technology affect your business?
- Learning resources. What type of knowledge is valuable to your practice, and how do you get it?
- Legal issues. What are the legal issues and regulations that affect your practice?
- Leadership. Who is the best person to lead, and where does that person fit into your business structure?

ACTION ITEMS

Are we too busy? There are so many books on being overworked and overstressed and about how to perform our tasks more efficiently. Many people do feel constantly overworked, whereas others are able to balance many balls and not feel stressed. What's the difference?

Often it's focusing on what really matters. Often we find 20 percent of our work is particularly important and what we need to do. The other 80 percent doesn't make that much difference. The question is: how can we develop a system whereby we do the important things first and minimize other, time-absorbing tasks that aren't as important?

It could be we're tracking too much data and processing too much information. The computer has created a situation that can be both constructive and destructive. Often we don't really need 90 percent of the information we get, but it's in front of us, so we think it's important. What information do we really need, and how do we screen out the rest of it?

Every day there are things we need to do that we hadn't planned. How can we get these done and still find the time for the important things? Is there a way to save a trip by combining two or three things? It's such a wonderful feeling at the end of the day to say you've done what you had to and didn't overtax yourself. It's wonderful to have a better attitude toward everything we do, because we've done it all with grace and pleasure, rather than by being stressed and overwhelmed.

Time Management

Time management has less to do with controlling time than with controlling events, according to Hyrum W. Smith, founder of the Franklin Quest Co. (now FranklinCovey), a time management firm. Smith says the secret of controlling events is to relate them to your personal values.[2]

Where do you want to spend time, and what do you want to do? Stephen R. Covey, author of *The Seven Habits of Highly Effective People*, suggests you list your most important values, then organize your schedule around these values. He then recommends breaking things down further into "urgent" and "important."[3]

There'll always be interruptions and demands in a business. The key to peace of mind is letting your values direct your schedule. In other words, schedule your priorities.

Covey lists three generations of time management. The first advises you to go with the flow but keep track of the things you do, checking off items on a list as you accomplish them. The second is planning and preparation: making appointments, identifying deadlines, and noting where meetings are held. The third is planning, prioritizing, and controlling. After spending time clarifying your values, you are asked to set long-, medium-, and short-term goals to obtain these values.

Do you really believe time management puts you in control? We live in the real world with real people who cannot be controlled. Does time management make you more efficient? Of course. You get more done, faster. But ask yourself if it's in the right direction. Plugging in your values isn't the whole answer, because values don't necessarily have anything to do with quality of life.

Covey says: "Traditional time management focuses on getting what you want and not letting anything get in the way." Other people are seen either as resources or obstacles, and relationships are transactional as opposed to transformational. He suggests that a fourth generation of time management is called for: knowing what's important, instead of simply responding to what's urgent.

This fourth generation of time management is most closely attuned to today's business management theories. Says Covey, "You manage things, but you must lead people."

Benchmarking

> *Benchmarking is the continuous process of measuring products, services, and practices against the toughest competitors or those companies recognized as industry leaders.*
>
> — DAVID KEARNS,
> FORMER CEO OF XEROX

Benchmarking and other management programs provide a system and structure to create the best operating procedures. It's possible to create a good system of management through inspiration, trial and error, and luck. You can have a firm that works well without having studied any specific management program.

But in benchmarking, you build on your own past successes and learn from the success of others. In any benchmarking or management plan, make sure the project has a clear focus.

Benchmarking lets you know where your firm stands in relation to the best in the industry. Benchmarking creates a fast-learning culture dedicated to continuous improvement. It supports strategic planning and helps accomplish organizational restructuring. Benchmarking works. It has a proven track record in firms such as Motorola, General Electric, Ford, and Xerox. It provides external reference points so your strategic planning isn't the equivalent of flying blind.

Study the Competition

Study your competition. It may point you toward a new segment of the market, or steer you away from it. Studying the competition is simply being aware of the movement in your market.

If a competing firm is so good at a specialty that it can perform the work better and less expensively than you could, it might be wise to stay out of that area of business unless you're willing to make an equal or greater investment.

Looking at whom your competition chooses as partners can be revealing. You may want to use some of the same consultants, because they have a track record in working with designers. Then again, the relationship between the outside professionals and the competition may be so strong that you need to look elsewhere for potential team members.

Who in your firm should study the competition? It makes sense to let your newest employee shop another store or office. But it takes someone with a knowledge of your business to really understand what the competition is doing. Ideally, this person will also know people within the competing firm from previous work associations and can speak with them. In the end, it may take everyone in your firm to gather information you or the team leader will analyze.

Some information about your competition can be found in databases accessible via the Internet and in newspapers, magazines, and other public records. Newspapers and magazines often list projects awarded to firms including details such as the square footage of the space and the nature of the projects. Installation stories can tell you how a design firm handles a specific problem. A company's stated philosophy of business is generally part of any profile in the business pages of the newspaper. Sometimes the society pages provide clues as to which designers are allied with which potential clients.

You also learn about your competition by attending meetings of professional organizations and by speaking with other competitors. Clients will often tell you how much they like a project, what worked, and what didn't. They may also tell you what it's like to work with your competition.

Workaholics

As reported in "Trend Letter,"[4] Stewart Friedman and Sharon Lobel at the Wharton School point out that a happy workaholic chooses to be at work. Many people enjoy their field so much that they really thrive on dedicating all their energies to it. This type of workaholism isn't necessarily destructive; on the contrary, it can build an industry. Often people have periods of workaholism lasting several months, during which they really concentrate on a project and want to get it accomplished. This can prove to be one of the happiest and most productive times of their lives.

Happy workaholics know their priorities and their own styles, and they admit they'd rather be working than doing anything else. Many companies are supporting "happy workaholism" by permitting people to work the hours they want to work. Other employees who don't want to work long hours because they have other obligations are now permitted to work less. Workaholics, on the other hand, are happy to be working; they just love it. It's so easy to spot the difference between someone who has to work and someone who chooses to. Fortunately, business structures today support people who are passionate and obsessive about what they do.

Notes

1. Jerry Porras, et. al. *Success Built to Last: Creating a Life that Matters.* Upper Saddle River, NJ: Reed Business Information, 2007.
2. Hyrum W. Smith. "Simple Secrets of Time Management," *Boardroom Reports*, April 1, 1994, p. 13.
3. Stephen Covey. *Success Magazine*, special book bonus excerpt, April 1994.
4. Stewart Friedman and Sharon Lobel. "Trend Letter," Briefings Publishing Group, March 2007.

THE DESIGN SPIRIT

Catch the spirit, or catch the bus.

We know the power of our design spirit. How can we pass this spirit on to our clients?

One thing is certain; you can't pass on the spirit if you're not willing to demonstrate it in every move.

People today are attracted to those who have direction and are able to communicate their enthusiasm.

Interior design has a power and an excitement like nothing else in the world. If you don't love your work, do something about it. Go to a seminar. Hire a coach. Learn why you don't like it, or get out of the field.

Remember that special teacher who explained things better than anyone else? Interior designers should want to be that special "teacher" who inspires as he or she explains and informs.

People follow examples. How do you live? Do you exemplify the word "designer"? Look at yourself first. Is your home your haven? Does it suit you? My private space is austere but peaceful, like the art of Japanese flower arranging. Clients think it's really "me."

Is your business really *you*? Be honest with yourself. We must know our field and how we fit into this sacred discipline of design. We are the high priests and with this responsibility comes great opportunity—a chance to make everyone's life more artistic, to give pleasure to a child, the aged, to everyone our work touches!

Express love and caring in the way you design. Help your clients show caring by creating an interior that speaks to all who enter.

How do you feel when you wake up in the morning? How do you treat yourself? Is the vision you see from your bed an experience that establishes your spirit for the day? You are affected by design as much as your clients are.

Today, business is based on high-tech humanism and relationships. We use technology to reduce the time and effort we spend on repetitive tasks so that we have more time to spend building the human part of our business. You're part of a community. In this world of the impersonal, we like to be supported, liked, and loved by those around us. This is probably more important than ever before. We expect this human element in the businesses we support. They're part of our neighborhood.

Interiors are motivation; they speak louder than voices. People are searching for spiritual experiences. Environments featuring art and design can provide those experiences. All of us have a real need and craving that interior designers can fill.

As a human factors specialist, I've learned to fill physical needs first. But when I interview clients many years later, they will say, Yes, the space worked. But it's the emotional experience they remember and treasure.

Your clients will have only the best, if they catch your spirit.

POSTSCRIPT

The design industry today is an extremely exciting and stimulating place in which to invest one's life. It's also chaotic and terrifying, but mostly exhilarating. The industry is full of opportunities.

No one has all the answers. I hope this book will stimulate every designer and every professional in allied fields to reexamine his or her work and invest in the opportunities available to us. It's time to recognize that designers are the leaders of tomorrow. We are creating change. We have a strong base of knowledge, a great spirit, and a soul. Interior design has the power to change lives. Use that power responsibly.

BOOK LIST

Abercrombie, Stanley. *A Philosophy of Interior Design*. New York: Harper and Row, 1990.

Belasco, James A. *Teaching the Elephant to Dance: Empowering Change in Your Organization*. New York: Crown, 1990.

Bennis, Warren G. *On Becoming a Leader*. New York: Addison-Wesley, 1989.

—— *On Becoming a Leader*. Chicago: Nightingale-Conant Corporation, 1991. (tape)

—— *An Invented Life: Reflections on Leadership and Change*. Reading, MA: Addison-Wesley, 1993.

Blanchard, Ken. *Leading at a Higher Level*. New York: Prentice Hall, 2007.

Block, Peter. *Stewardship: The Triumph of Service over Self-Interest or Choosing Service Over Self-Interest*. San Francisco: Berrett-Koehler, 1993.

Brooks, David. *Bobos in Paradise: The Upper Class and How They Got There*. New York: Simon and Schuster, 2000.

Carnegie, Dale, and Associates, Inc. *The Leader in You*. New York: Simon and Schuster, 1994.

Covey, Stephen. *The Seven Habits of Highly Effective People: Restoring the Character Ethic*. New York: Simon and Schuster, 1983.

—— *Principle-Centered Leadership*. New York: Summit Books, 1991.

Covey, Stephen, et. al. *The Speed of Trust: The One Thing that Changes Everything*. New York: Simon and Schuster, 2006.

Davis, Stanley M. *Future Perfect*. New York: Addison-Wesley, 1987.

—— *Lessons from the Future: Making Sense of a Blurred World from the World's Leading Futurist*. Oxford: Capstone Publishing Ltd. (John Wiley & Sons Co.), 2001.

DePree, Hugh D. *Business as Unusual.* Zeeland, MI: Herman Miller, Inc., 1986.

DePree, Max. *Leadership Is an Art.* New York: Doubleday, 1989.

Drucker, Peter F. *Managing a Non-Profit Organization: Principles and Practices.* New York: HarperCollins, 1990.

—— *Post-Capitalist Society.* New York: HarperBusiness, 1993.

—— *Management Challenges for the 21st Century.* New York: HarperCollins, 1999.

Edelston, Martin and Marion Buhagiar. *I-Power: The Secrets of Great Business in Bad Times.* Fort Lee, NJ: Barricade Books, 1992.

Enriquez, Juan.. *Probing as The Future Catches You.* New York: Crown Publishing, 2000.

Florida, Richard. *The Rise of the Creative Class.* New York: Basic Books, 2002.

—— *The Flight of the Creative Class.* New York: HarperCollins, 2006.

Gardner, Howard. *Five Minds for the Future.* Boston: Harvard Business School Press, 2006.

Gladwell, Malcolm. *The Tipping Point: How Little Things Can Make a Big Difference.* Little, Brown and Co., 2000.

—— *Blink: The Power of Thinking Without Thinking.* Little, Brown and Co., 2005.

Goldratt, Eliyahu M., and Jeff Cox. *The Goal.* St. Paul, MN: Penguin-High Bridge Audio, 1992.

Godin, Seth. *Small is the New Big.* New York: Penguin Group, 2006.

Hall, Edward T. *The Hidden Dimension.* New York: Doubleday-Anchor, 1966.

Handy, Charles. *The Age of Paradox.* Boston, MA: Harvard Business School Press, 1994.

Hammer, Michael, and James Champy. *Reengineering the Corporation: A Manifesto for Business Revolution.* New York: Harper Business, 1993.

Hickman, Craig R. *Mind of a Manager, Soul of a Leader.* New York: John Wiley, 1990.

—— *The Oz Principle: Getting Results Through Individual and Organizational Accountability.* Englewood Cliffs, NJ: Prentice-Hall 1994.

Johnson, Lisa. *Mind Your X's and Y's: Satisfying the 10 Cravings of a New Generation of Consumers.* New York: Free Press, 2006.

Krugman, Paul. *The Accidental Theorist and Other Dispatches from the Dismal Science.* New York: W.W. Norton & Co., 1999.

Maxwell, John C. *The Difference Maker: Making Your Attitude Your Greatest Asset.* Nashville: Nelson Business, 2006.

Michelli, Joseph A., Ph.D. *The Starbucks Experience: 5 Principles for Turning Ordinary Into Extraordinary.* New York: McGraw Hill, 2006.

Naisbitt, John. *Global Paradox: The Bigger the World Economy, The More Powerful Its Smallest Players.* New York: William Morrow, 1994.

Naisbitt, John, and Patricia Aburdene. *Megatrends 2000: Ten New Directions for the 1990s.* New York: William Morrow, 1994.

Ott, John N. *Light, Radiation and You: How to Stay Healthy.* Greenwich: Devin Adair Publishers, 1982.

Peppers, Don, and Martha Rogers. *The One-to-One Future: Building Relationships, One Customer at a Time.* New York: Currency Doubleday, 1993.

Peters, Thomas J. *Thriving on Chaos: A Handbook for a Management Revolution.* New York: Alfred A. Knopf, 1987.

—— *Liberation Management: Necessary Disorganization for the Nanosecond Nineties.* New York: Alfred A. Knopf, 1992.

—— *The Seminar: Crazy Times Call for Crazy Organizations.* New York: Vintage Books, 1994.

Pile, John. *Interior Design.* New York: Abrams, 1988.

Pink, Daniel H. *A Whole New Mind.* New York: Penguin Group, 2006.

Porras, Jerry, et. al. *Success Built to Last: Creating a Life that Matters.* Upper Saddle River, NJ: Reed Business Information, 2007.

Senge, Peter M. *The Fifth Discipline: The Art and Practice of the Learning Organization.* New York: Currency Doubleday, 1990.

Senge, Peter M., et. al. *The Fifth Discipline Fieldbook: Strategies for Building a Learning Organization.* New York: Currency Doubleday, 1994.

Stanley, Thomas J. *Marketing to the Affluent.* Homewood, IL: Dow Jones-Irwin, 1988.

—— *Selling to the Affluent.* Homewood, IL: Business One Irwin, 1991.

Toffler, Alvin. *Powershift: Knowledge, Wealth and Violence at the Edge of the 21st Century.* New York: Bantam Books, 1990.

Toffler, Alvin and Heidi. *Revolutionary Wealth: How It Was Created and How It Will Change Our Lives.* New York: Alfred A. Knopf, 2006.

Trout, Jack. *The Power of Simplicity.* New York: McGraw Hill, 1999.

Waterman, Robert H., Jr. *What America Does Right: Learning from Companies that Put People First.* New York: W.W. Norton, 1994.

Whiton, Sherill. *Elements of Interior Design and Decoration.* New York: Lippincott, 1944.

DESIGNERS' BUSINESS FORUM

The Designers' Business Forum is a program developed to help designers, architects, and other creative professionals establish their best opportunities in today's business environment. Their businesses are very much needed and valued today, but they require a special structure and process to make them successful.

The forum uses a design process—a system that creative people find familiar and user-friendly. It considers each person's special abilities and works to develop the best opportunities for growth and success for that individual's firm.

The program is highly participatory and interactive. You meet with other designers to share experiences. You benefit from regular personal contact with other creative people. Regular support is available to assist you with daily problems and the process of growing your business. Whenever you have a question or problem, call us first. We will assist you or find support for you. You are not alone.

If you are interested in growing your firm, you will enjoy the forum. You will have the opportunity to do better work, experience an easier process, earn better income, and have more time for the pleasures of life.

Our goal is to raise the level of the design profession. Join us. Let's make it happen.

For more information on this program or other issues, contact:

Mary V. Knackstedt
2901 North Front Street
Harrisburg, PA 17110
Phone: 717-238-7548
Fax: 717-233-7374
E-mail: maryknackstedt@aol.com

INDEX

Books from Allworth Press

Allworth Press is an imprint of Allworth Communications, Inc. Selected titles are listed below.

How to Start and Operate Your Own Design Firm: A Guide for Interior Designers and Architects, Second Edition
by Albert W. Rubeling, Jr., FAIA (paperback, 6 × 9, 256 pages, $24.95)

Business and Legal Forms for Interior Designers
by Tad Crawford and Eva Doman Bruck (paperback, 8 ½ × 11, 240 pages, $29.95)

The Interior Designer's Guide to Pricing, Estimating, and Budgeting
by Theo Stephan Williams (paperback, 6 × 9, 208 pages, $19.95)

How to Think Like a Great Graphic Designer
by Debbie Millman (paperback, 6 × 9, 248 pages, $24.95)

The Graphic Designer's Guide to Better Business Writing
by Barbara Janoff and Ruth Cash-Smith (paperback, 6 × 9, 256 pages, $19.95)

Creating the Perfect Design Brief: How to Manage Design for Strategic Advantage
by Peter L. Phillips (paperback, 6 × 9, 224 pages, $19.95)

The Graphic Design Business Book
by Tad Crawford (paperback, 6 × 9, 256 pages, $24.95)

Graphic Designer's Guide to Clients: How to Make Clients Happy and Do Great Work
by Ellen Shapiro (paperback, 6 × 9, 256 pages, $19.95)

AIGA Professional Practices in Graphic Design, Second Edition
edited by Tad Crawford (paperback, 6 × 9, 336 pages, $29.95)

Designing Logos: The Process of Creating Logos That Endure
by Jack Gernsheimer (paperback, 8 ½ × 10, 208 pages, $35.00)

Designing Effective Communications: Creating Contexts for Clarity and Meaning
edited by Jorge Frascara (paperback, 6 × 9, 304 pages, 100 b&w illustrations, $24.95)

To request a free catalog or order books by credit card, call 1-800-491-2808. To see our complete catalog on the World Wide Web, or to order online for a 20 percent discount, you can find us at ***www.allworth.com***.